For Michael,
who stayed in Jerusalem

WHERE MOUNTAINS ROAR

Also by Lesley Hazleton

Israeli Women (1978)

WHERE MOUNTAINS ROAR

A PERSONAL
REPORT FROM THE
SINAI AND NEGEV
DESERT

by Lesley Hazleton

Holt, Rinehart and Winston
New York

Published by Holt, Rinehart and Winston, 383 Madison Avenue, New York,
New York 10017.
Published simultaneously in Canada by Holt, Rinehart and Winston of Canada,
Limited.

Library of Congress Cataloging in Publication Data
Hazleton, Lesley.
Where mountains roar.
Bibliography: p. 223.
1. Sinaitic Peninsula—Description and travel.
2. Negev—Description and travel. 3. Hazleton, Lesley.
I. Title.
DS110.5.H37 1980   953'.1   79-22009
ISBN 0-03-045321-6

Designer: Margaret Wagner
Map: Bernhard H. Wagner
Printed in the United States of America

Endpaper illustration: David Roberts. "Ascent of the Lower Range of Sinai."
From *The Holy Land from Drawings Made on the Spot*, 1855.

Portions of *Where Mountains Roar* have appeared, in slightly modified form, in *Geo*,
Quest '79, and *The New York Review of Books*.

Acknowledgments

The rules of desert courtesy and hospitality are still alive and well in the Sinai and Negev, and because the desert is so sparsely populated, one remembers human encounters in it with a special clarity and appreciation. Particular thanks are due to those who afforded me the means and the ways to explore the desert. Chief among these is Professor Amos Richmond, head of the Desert Research Institute at Sde Boker, a campus of the Ben-Gurion University of the Negev, whose generous invitation to stay in the institute and use its facilities afforded me a superb "home base." Amir Edelman, head of the Sde Boker Field Station run by the Israel Society for the Protection of Nature, oversaw my introduction to the desert with an infectious enthusiasm, and his staff, in particular Mirav Hofi and Udi Shani, warmly gave of themselves and their time to become, in effect, my personal guides. Special thanks are due also to Lieutenant Colonel Ami Gluska, chief spokesman of the Israel Defense Forces in Jerusalem, for expediting my way in the Sinai and ensuring that the army extend me the maximum of courtesy and aid, and to Dr. Reuven Yagil of the Ben-Gurion University of the Negev for his guidance on the physiology of the camel.

The Beduin songs quoted in the chapter on camels are from "Poetry of the Desert" by Dr. Clinton Bailey, in *Ariel* magazine, No. 33–34, 1973, and the famous statement at the end of the Author's Note—"the wilderness holds answers to more questions than we yet know how to ask"—is from *This Is the American Earth* by Ansel Adams and Nancy Newhall, published by Ballantine/Sierra Club in 1971.

Contents

A map of the Sinai and Negev Desert appears on page 23.

Author's Note

In the spring of 1978, I left my home in Jerusalem to go south into the Sinai and Negev desert. Naïvely, as it now seems to me, I imagined that I would go into the desert and write of it as an observer. I had little idea then of the force of the desert or of how it would affect me. There was a certain diffuse fear that the coming year would somehow change me, but I struggled to ignore it. Fascinated by the desert but unwilling to face the depths of that fascination, I stubbornly set out to do what I had intended.

I could not. Slowly and unwillingly, I began to realize that it was no longer I who was shaping this book, directing my thoughts and perceptions, but the desert itself. And as this realization grew, so too the fear of it began to dissipate. Soon I welcomed this force of the desert, opening myself up to the changes it wrought on my seeing, my feeling, my writing.

No longer, it seemed, was it so important to know the desert in the academic sense—to go everywhere in it, know the name of every plant and every wadi. Now there was a different kind of knowing, far closer to the biblical sense of the word. By allowing the desert to enter into me, and by entering into the desert, I found a level of intimacy and respect that transcended academic detail to reach through to the essence of the desert itself and to the essence of my own being.

And so when I returned to Jerusalem, to write in this mountain city of stone, I wrote above all of the experience of the desert. And although I called on all the resources that could deepen my experience and understanding—on the disciplines of geography, geology, anthropology, history, botany, biology—I found that the desert was more than the sum of the ways in which it can be studied. It is a vast living world unto itself, a world beyond our limited human concepts of time and space.

The Sinai and Negev, the thirty-thousand-square-mile land link between Africa and Asia, is the holiest desert in the world. It is also the most battle-scarred desert in the world. Never has any desert called forth so much awe or so much blood. I had intended to capture this desert and put it into a book. Instead, the desert captured me. In retrospect, it seems inevitable. This is no longer a book about the desert, but more, I feel, a book *of* the desert—a desert book for those who sense that "the wilderness holds answers to more questions than we yet know how to ask."

Jerusalem, June 1979

WHERE MOUNTAINS ROAR

Prologue

When I studied geography as a child in England, it seemed that half the globe was colored a deep pink, meaning that all these lands were part of the British Empire. That was in the early fifties, and the Sinai and Negev, like much of the Middle East, was still part of this deep pink empire, for the manufacturers of children's globes take some time to adjust to reality, and the atlases we used in school had been handed down through at least a generation of bare-kneed, school-tied English children. The existence of political boundaries between such newfangled entities as Israel, Egypt, and Jordan was apparently considered a matter to be fathomed only by the next generation.

There was a reassuring sense of solidity in all that deep pink. Britain of the early fifties had not quite realized that it had lost an empire. We still recited Rudyard Kipling's more patriotic poems, with their visions of a strong and sturdy world order emanating from this tiny island on the fringe of the Atlantic. Britannia still ruled the waves in our imaginations, and we warmed to Rupert Brooke's selfless image of the soldier:

> If I should die, think only this of me:
> That there's some corner of a foreign field
> That is for ever England.

We were the first of what would later be called "the postwar generation." Many of us were conceived before Hiroshima

1

and born after peace was declared. And because we had no direct knowledge of World War II, it was perhaps easier for us than for our elders to come to terms with the gradual disappearance of the deep pink from the globe as we grew into adulthood. The last decades of the Empire were too recent to be history, and too distant to involve us. We thought of ourselves as English, not British.

Then in 1966 I came to live in the Middle East and saw my English manners and customs, even my English accent, gradually fade over the years in the clear warm air of Jerusalem. There were still flashes of insight into what the Empire was like. Lying under the palm trees by the swimming pool of the King David Hotel, for instance, facing the flags and arched portals of the French consulate and Jesuit Institute to the north, it would have needed only a white-jacketed waiter bearing a gin and tonic for me to be persuaded that the clock had been turned back fifty years. But for the most part, the hectic vitality of modern Israeli life drove England from my mind. Or so I thought.

Certainly nothing could be farther from England's "green and pleasant land" than the desert, whose stark majesty beckoned to the south and east of this ancient city of stone. Early in 1968 I thought to obey that summons, and went down to the central Negev to explore the possibility of lecturing in psychology at the Sde Boker teachers' seminar. But I was still afraid, I think, to commit myself to living in the midst of such vastness; I sought again the refuge of the city walls. The years passed, and I abandoned my work in psychology for the constant present tense of journalism. Perhaps I gained courage in those years, or perhaps the desert had implanted its imperative in me too deeply to be ignored. Whichever, when I left Jerusalem in 1978 to go to Sde Boker as a guest of the new Desert Research Institute, my home base for what was to be a few months but became nearly a year, it seemed an entirely natural move. It was practically ten years to the day since I had first considered living in the desert. I put aside journalism for the time being and had the luxury of time and freedom from other commitments to explore my affinity with the desert—the luxury of the writer. I was coming fresh to the desert, I thought, unencumbered by past or present concerns. But I found that the desert too has a past. And so it was that I rediscovered the British Empire there.

It could be that the Britisher in me was less dormant than I had supposed. Or it may be simply that I love the smell of the old books that tell of empire, and the texture of old engravings. Or—and this I think is closest to the truth—it could be that I *wanted* to turn back the clock and see this desert when it was still wild and unknown, when there were no roads and air routes, when the Beduin were still nomadic raiders, and when a handful of iconoclastic explorers were the only Westerners to venture here.

It was these explorers who brought the British Empire alive for me. For most of the explorers of the Middle East's deserts have been Englishmen. At first, in all innocence, I began to suspect something inherent in the British character that brought these men into the desert—an adventurous trait that could develop only within an upper-class English upbringing in an age of empire, the kind of upbringing that instilled a sense of superiority and security in even the most unlikely circumstances. But as I read on through the nineteenth- and early-twentieth-century accounts, I began to grasp the political realities behind their adventures. The explorers were the forerunners of the Empire. They were often the first "white men" to set foot in unknown territory, and they brought back with them detailed accounts of the terrain and of the population and, most important, maps.

I doubt if anyone can read their accounts without being deeply impressed by the sheer Britishness of their style and attitude, by that undaunted sense of privilege and rightness in being British that has now long been out of style but that was perfectly in accord with the Britain of the Empire.

Four of these accounts struck a particular chord for me. It

was as though the sparseness of the desert itself had forced these men into an unsparing revelation of themselves and their Britishness, and forced me, also, into a reappraisal of my own Britishness. These four accounts range from the ruthless egocentricity of the Orientalist E. H. Palmer to the deep humanity and humility of the traveler C. M. Doughty, from a Britishness that makes me cringe in rejection to one that I can wholeheartedly embrace, saying "Yes, this is the Britishness that informed my childhood." And when I examined my reactions more closely, I realized that the closer such travelers were to the desert—the more they came to it for the desert itself rather than out of loyalty to the idea of empire—the more I found in them the positive values of my own Britishness.

The desert is an unsparing environment, and in it, the dry wit and aplomb for which Britishers are renowned can no longer hide a lack of humanity. Those who respect the desert respect its inhabitants, too, and that respect is the basis of their humanity. Where respect for the desert is lacking, there is no humanity to be found. So that when all the dash and style of the British veneer is done with, it is in their relationships with the Beduin that these men finally reveal themselves and their Empire—and what the desert was for them.

Professor Edward Henry Palmer's declared concern was "the connection between sacred history and sacred geography," to which end he joined the British Ordnance Survey Expedition to the Peninsula of Sinai in 1868. The expedition was first to identify Mount Sinai and then to survey all possible routes of the Exodus from Egypt. This remarkable exercise in biblical geography was sponsored by none other than the British army—specifically, the Royal Engineering Corps, which seconded two captains to head the party and four noncommissioned officers as manpower.

No one has established beyond doubt the identity of the

"real" Mount Sinai. Jebel Musa is generally acknowledged as the true peak, and is accepted by all three of the religions in which it plays a role, partly because there is little religious desire to prove what is essentially unprovable. Biblical archaeologists still argue the point, as they do the route of the Exodus, but then that is their job. If Jebel Musa has to have a contender for the title of Mount Sinai, however, Jebel Serbal, whose striking triple peak dominates the western part of the Sinai mountain range, is certainly a good choice.

Palmer's party proposed to solve the problem of which mountain is the true one by mapping both Jebel Musa and Jebel Serbal—on a scale of six inches to the mile. Carrying out such a detailed survey was no simple matter, as Palmer wryly made clear:

"There was . . . no wood to be procured, and cairns, instead of poles or flagstaffs, had to be erected on the various points of observation; these required whitewashing, in order to make them sufficiently conspicuous; and one or the other of the officers could have been often seen clambering up some precipitous crag, and holding the whitewash pot in his mouth, with the pleasant conviction that a false step might cause him to spill the precious contents and render his day's labor useless.

"It was a very common experience, too, for us to reach the top of a peak in a state of profuse perspiration, and five minutes later to stand there so benumbed with cold that we could scarcely hold a pencil, or manipulate the screws of an instrument. The jolting over the rough, loose boulders which do duty for paths is also very trying, especially in a steep descent; you hop from stone to stone like an animated cricket-ball, until every joint seems dislocated and every sinew strained, while occasionally a piece of rock bounds gracefully away from under your feet, and you come down heavily upon your occiput with a piece of sharp granite in the small of your back."

The maps drawn up by this intrepid band of whitewashers

are beautifully shaded to show the ruggedness and imposing grandeur of the two mountains. The final decision fell in favor of Jebel Musa, less because of any feature of the mountain itself than because there is no open space near Serbal large enough to have held all the children of Israel in camp.

But behind the apparently picayune interest in which mountain was which, there lay a coldly calculated purpose. For the main work of the expedition was a systematic survey of the interior of the Sinai, under cover of establishing the route of the Exodus. The scale of their maps was to be two miles to the inch, "including all the principal routes and main geographical features in the western half of the Peninsula." Although Palmer never clarified the British army's interest in either Mount Sinai or the Exodus, the maps drawn up by the expedition were to be invaluable in later years. In Palmer's time, the status of the Sinai was most unclear. The Ottoman and the British empires met somewhere in the peninsula, though exactly where was not known. It was, after all, mere desert. It was not until 1906 that a joint commission of Turkish and British officers came from Jerusalem and Cairo to establish the line that would differentiate the Sinai from the Negev, everything northeast of that line being accorded to Turkish domain, and everything southwest of it, to British. But even then the line was a mere paper reality, as the British were to prove in 1917 when they drove the Turks up out of the Negev and out of most of the Middle East—using, among other maps, those drawn up by Palmer's expedition.

Palmer returned to the Middle East one year after the Ordnance Survey Expedition to extend the map northward, teaming up with an archaeologist for a journey through the northern Sinai and the Negev. But in his account of both expeditions, *The Desert of the Exodus*, the wit and style of his writing eventually reveal a shallowness of perception of the desert. And that shallowness, in an Englishman of the Empire, easily became callousness.

Palmer's excellent command of Arabic served him well in

establishing contact with the Beduin, who guided and sometimes hosted him and his colleagues. But there were still sticky
situations with hostile Beduin whom he did not know. A
goodly dose of plain courage, a thick streak of stubbornness,
and a well-developed sense of humor got him through such
times but did nothing to lessen his contempt for the Beduin.
He called them "a terrible scourge," claiming that wherever
the Beduin goes, "he brings with him ruin, violence and ne-
glect. To call him 'a son of the desert' is a misnomer; half the
desert owes its existence to him, and many a fertile plain from
which he has driven its useful and industrious inhabitants
becomes in his hands a parched and barren wilderness. . . .

"I do not advocate a war of extermination against the
Bedawin, because I do not think it policy to destroy so much
muscle which might be made serviceable to the community,
and I have still, even in the days of mitrailleuses, some
old-fashioned notions about the sacredness of human life, but
I would put an end to their existence qua Bedawin. . . . If the
military authorities were to make systematic expeditions
against these tribes, and take away from them every camel and
sheep which they possess, they would no longer be able to
roam over the deserts, but would be compelled to settle down
to agricultural pursuits or starve. The superior advantages
which the peaceful agriculturalist would then possess over
them would curb their unreasonable pride, and the necessity
for keeping pace with him, if they wished to live at all, would
bring out the resources of their undoubtedly keen intellects.
They might thus be tamed and turned into useful members of
the community. Such a plan would probably entail some
hardships and injustices at first, but a virulent disease requires
a strong remedy, and we must not wince at the application of
the cautery to cure the plague."

Perhaps Palmer was incapable of anything other than this
repulsive response to the hospitality and help he had received
from so many Beduin. He was an advocate of the Empire as
the harbinger of civilization, and the Beduin, to him, were

anticivilization. For like so many well-bred Englishmen of his time, he could admit of no form of civilization other than his own. The desert itself partook of this anticivilization, and Palmer described its extremes of heat and cold and its aridity with repellent force, harping on the word *sterility*. His harsh view of the human and natural environment permeated even his descriptions of the desert's undeniable beauty. "Nature seems to show that in her most barren and uninviting moods she can be exquisitely beautiful still," he wrote. The desert was beautiful only despite itself.

Palmer returned to the desert in the service of his idea of civilization. It was to be his death. In 1881, he resigned his post as Lord Almoner's Reader in Arabic at St. John's College, Cambridge, and was dispatched to the Sinai. His mission was to contact the Beduin and persuade them against joining the rebellion against British rule in Egypt. To aid his powers of persuasion, he carried with him twenty thousand pounds in gold, a true fortune for that time. Since the news of his mission and the means by which he was to accomplish it spread quickly, he and his companions were scarcely the safest of travelers from the outset. Inevitably, they were ambushed and killed by Beduin, though whether solely for the gold or for political reasons as well was never established. It was an ironic death; in it, Palmer proved what he had said about the Beduin, and in it, the Beduin gained their revenge.

Eventually, the bodies were recovered, and Palmer and his two military escorts were buried in no less a place than St. Paul's Cathedral, London. In true-blue fashion, the plaque above their graves makes no mention of their foolishness, but reads: "In memory of three brave men . . . who when travelling on public duty into the Sinai Desert were treacherously and cruelly slain."

Compared to Palmer, Major Claude Scudamore Jarvis, CMG, OBE (Companion of the Most Excellent Order of St. Michael and St. George, and Officer of the Most Excellent Order of the British Empire), was a benign father figure. But this benign patriarchalism was merely the other face of the sense of invincible superiority that spawned Palmer's callousness.

Jarvis joined the service of the British High Commissioner in Egypt in 1918, and five years later became governor of the Sinai, a post he held until the Egyptians managed to get the British out, thirteen years later. Jarvis was an administrator, not an explorer, but he soon gained the respect of the Beduin under his aegis, partly because he was so unerringly British. The whimsy that led him to do much of his writing under the pen name of Rameses carried over into the books to which he signed his own name. For example, he dedicated *Three Deserts* to "the woman who goes East. In profound admiration of her selflessness in sharing the lot of the White Man Overseas, softening his hardships, easing his loneliness and making of his isolated bungalow a place 'that is for ever England.' " Tongue hard in cheek, and yet serious for all that. In *Desert and Delta* he took upon himself the unenviable task of defending the British custom of dressing for dinner—when alone in the desert.

"As a man who has perpetrated this particular form of idiocy, snobbery, 'Old School Tie-ism' or what you will, of dressing for dinner for eighteen years," he wrote, "I think it necessary therefore to make some form of apology or explanation for this extraordinary and stupid behavior." The main point of dressing for dinner, he argued, was to avoid "going slack," more commonly known at times as "going native." "I am not certain if one can call the character of the average Beduin a strong and compelling one, but the fact remains that in nine cases out of ten he leaves a far more indelible mark on his administrator than his administrator leaves on him. . . . No matter how he [the administrator] may have fought against it, the Arab has stamped him with the Beduin hallmark and he will find for the rest of his life that this queer nomad outlook will persist in all things. . . .

"It may be argued that the wearing of a black tie at night is a queer and petty method of fighting against this Beduin bewitchment, but it is a gesture, a definite stand in fact, against the very natural desire to let all details and routine go by the board. There is something so entirely British about the proceeding that unconsciously one regains every evening something of the Occident that has been lost or Orientalized during the day. . . . There is no necessity to wear that abomination of civilization the boiled shirt or a stiff collar—in any case they are unobtainable—but as one must bathe and change one may as well don a soft white shirt and collar and slip on an aged dinner jacket, or in hot weather a white drill imitation of the garment, for after all there is nothing so comfortable and easy as this particular cut."

Social reasons are no less important than those of personal maintenance. "If Master goes slack it is a most excellent excuse for this slackness extending to the kitchen." One can then find oneself in the most awkward situations. "No matter how well trained one's servants may be, a month of haphazard waiting at table serving scratch meals is quite sufficient for them to forget completely the routine of an ordinary dinner, and one's guests will have whiskey poured into their sherry glasses with the soup course, soda water squirted into the port, and other enormities will occur giving definite proof to the visitors that this is the first time in one's life one has attempted to give a dinner-party." Make no mistake—it was on such niceties, no matter how humorously stated, that the social formula of an empire was maintained.

Most of Jarvis's everyday work was in contact with the Beduin, about whom he fancied himself freed of illusions. "I am sometimes taken to task as a man who has 'let the side down,'" he wrote, "in that having been an Arab administrator for eighteen years, I have had the bad taste to come home and explode romantic myths by criticizing the Arab race. . . . Such is the natural and intriguing charm of the Arab people that the man who has lived too long among them is apt to become so enthralled by the race that he sees everything from an entirely Arab point of view, and he gives vent to his feelings and opinions so vehemently in the Press and on the lecture platform that the people of this country and the United States have come to believe that the Arab is a paragon of all the virtues—a blend in fact of Richard Coeur de Lion and Saladin with the acquired wisdom and restraint of Mr. Asquith thrown in"—a politely pointed barb at the journalist Lowell Thomas, who lectured throughout the 1920s and 1930s on T. E. Lawrence as "Lawrence of Arabia," making a small fortune out of doing so.

Jarvis's criticism of the Beduin had none of the vindictiveness displayed by Palmer, being limited mainly to the point that the Beduin were neither the brave fighters of legend nor hard workers. He maintained a similarly "no-nonsense" attitude toward the desert as a whole. Long paeans to the beauty of the desert were not for him. "I have no dislike of deserts," he wrote. "I have lived in them for eighteen years and can appreciate their vastness, the purity of their keen air, their beauty at dawn and sunset and their wonderful starlit nights. At the same time, I see no reason why a desert should be allowed to remain a desert if it can be turned into anything else." It was this line of thinking that was to make Jarvis one of the few British Mandate figures popular among the Israelis, who created an ideology of cultivating the desert.

The spot that Jarvis chose for his attempt to turn the desert into something else was Ein Gedeirat (Kadesh Barnea), where a perennial spring has attracted weary desert travelers for thousands of years. But there was a problem. The Gedeirat spring created a series of pools in which Anopheles mosquitoes bred. The first part of Jarvis's project was thus the technical one of cleaning up the water flow. He had a dam and a series of channels built to spread the water evenly over as large an area as possible; some parts of this system were reconstructions of the ancient Byzantine waterworks on the site. The second part of his project was far more difficult—

convincing the Gedeirat Beduin that it would be worth their while to invest the labor required to make the wadi into an orchard. It is to Jarvis's credit not only that he achieved this aim, but also that he did not totally despair of the Beduin during it, for as he put it, "the Beduin does not become a cultivator without a strong struggle against enslavement." Jarvis insisted and persuaded, and where words failed, brought in skilled labor from El Arish to lay out the gardens. By 1936, when he left, the "Gedeirat irrigation scheme" had been in operation for twelve years, and some three hundred acres boasted hundreds of olive trees and vines, where before there had been six acres of cultivated land and a malaria-infested valley. Today, it is still more beautiful, with pomegranate and other fruit trees and even—miracle of miracles in the desert—grass.

These twelve years gave Jarvis what he called "the most complete satisfaction in the world, of turning barren desert into a producing land." Though the Gedeirat project was to the material benefit entirely of the Beduin, he admitted that "my efforts were not entirely altruistic, for one gets an enormous kick out of defeating the desert, and there is far more satisfaction to be obtained from half a dozen olive trees one has forced to grow where nothing grew before than from a wonderful rock garden one has created in England from plants supplied by the nurseryman."

If any nurseryman in England ever supplied T. E. Lawrence with plants, they must surely have been thornbushes. Yet in their different ways the governor turned gardener and the soldier-spy turned legend served the same interest—England's interest in maintaining control of the Suez Canal and of all access to it. But where Jarvis's method was a benign paternalism, Lawrence's was a spirited identification that turned what was originally manipulation of the Beduin into leadership.

There was nothing genial about Lawrence. He wrote with a sharp honesty—an unusual honesty for an Englishman—

revealing what he knew to be callousness combined with recklessness, two of the features that enabled him to attain the status of legend among the Beduin.

That legend is still very much alive. Lawrence never went farther south into the Sinai than the line between Suez and Eilat, yet his name lives there, as I discovered when reading *The Seven Pillars of Wisdom*. I found it a hard book to read. I was repelled by the deliberate description of only the harshest conditions of the desert and by Lawrence's own personality no less than by his gross overromanticization of the Beduin, whom he dubbed "my Arabs." Though it was fascinating, it was also slow going, and so I toted the book around with me for some weeks.

During that time, on a hot day toward the end of the summer, I was in Firan—an oasis of date palms southeast of Suez. My traveling companions had gone on down the wadi and I, wanting to be alone a little, had stayed behind on a small wooden bench outside a Beduin shack where coffee was served, to be by myself and to read. The heat must have addled my brains somewhat, for I should have known better than to think I could be alone in such circumstances. Hardly had the others gone than I was surrounded by Beduin boys, all of them clamoring to know what I was reading and why. My rudimentary Arabic combined with their rudimentary Hebrew established a status quo whereby they would leave me in quiet for five minutes at a time, and then crowd in on me again. Finally I gave in and spent the rest of the afternoon vying with them on slingshots. But before closing the book, I showed them the photograph of Lawrence in it.

"Do you know who that is?"

They shook their heads dubiously. "Who?"

"That's an Englishman who fought with the Beduin. Do you know who?"

They thought. And then one of them, the eldest, suddenly lit up and jabbed his finger at the photograph. "That's el-Aurans," he said. "El-Aurans, and Feisal, together!"

The boy was twelve years old. It wasn't clear where he had heard about "el-Aurans," whether from his elders in the tribe or from Israeli archaeologists passing through. Whichever, he took great delight in tracing Lawrence's doings on the map, amazed at how large Arabia was compared to the Sinai and disappointed that Lawrence was never here, in this shady resting place nestled deep between the gaunt granite peaks of the Sinai.

Lawrence himself would have been disgusted by this scene. Aware of the growing legend about him, he felt guilty about it, as well he might, for he was serving two masters—the British and the Beduin. And the longer he fought with the Beduin, the stronger the conflict between the two masters became, for he was perfectly aware that the British were merely using the Beduin and the Arab revolt for their own purposes, in full cynicism. It led and could only lead to personal tragedy for Lawrence. And he was aware of this at the time.

"I was sent to these Arabs as a stranger," he wrote, "unable to think their thoughts or subscribe to their beliefs, but charged by duty to lead them forward and to develop to the highest any movement of theirs profitable to England in her war . . . Beduin ways were hard even for those brought up to them, and for strangers terrible: a death in life. When the march or labor ended I had no energy to record sensation, nor while it lasted any leisure to see the spiritual loveliness which sometimes came upon us by the way. In my notes, the cruel rather than the beautiful found place. We no doubt enjoyed more the rare moments of peace and forgetfulness; but I remember more the agony, the terrors, and the mistakes. Our life is not summed up in what I have written (there are things not to be repeated in cold blood for very shame); but what I have written was in and of our life. Pray God that men reading the story will not, for love of the glamor of strangeness, go out to prostitute themselves and their talents in serving another race."

It is when he talks of himself that Lawrence is most

poignant. And it is then that he reveals the terrible price of the legend, the reality behind the romantic image. "In my case, the efforts of these years to live in the dress of the Arabs, and to imitate their mental foundation, quitted me of my English self, and let me look at the West and its conventions with new eyes: they destroyed it all for me. At the same time I could not sincerely take on the Arab skin: it was an affectation only. Easily was a man made an infidel, but hardly might he be converted to another faith. I had dropped one form and not taken on the other, and was become like Mohammed's coffin in our legend, with a resultant feeling of intense loneliness in life, and a contempt, not for other men, but for all they do. Such detachment came at times to a man exhausted by prolonged physical effort and isolation. His body plodded on mechanically, while his reasonable mind left him, and from without looked down critically on him, wondering what that futile lumber did and why. Sometimes these selves would converse in the void; and then madness was very near, as I believe it would be near the man who could see things through the veils of two customs, two educations, two environments."

It was no love of the desert as such that led Lawrence into the Arab revolt. Though at times he described it as something near beautiful, his lyricism was reserved solely for the harshness of the desert, and for the pain it could inflict. He described marching "over monotonous, glittering sand; and over those worse stretches, *giaan*, of polished mud, nearly as white and smooth as laid paper, and often whole miles square. They blazed back the sun into our faces with glassy vigor, so we rode with its light raining direct arrows upon our heads, and its reflection glancing up from the ground through our inadequate eyelids. It was not a steady pressure, but a pain ebbing and flowing; at one time piling itself up and up till we nearly swooned; and then falling away coolly, in a moment of false shadow like a black web crossing the retina: these gave us a moment's breathing space to store new capacity for suffering, like the struggles to the surface of a drowning man."

Lawrence's complex neuroticism is far more fascinating than the genial eccentricity of Major Jarvis. Both got "a kick out of defeating the desert," but where for Jarvis this kick was expressed in planting olive trees, for Lawrence it became an extremely personal battle between the very basis of his soul and the extremes of the desert. Knowing that he took pleasure in pain, he tried to push the pain beyond the limits of even his own extreme pleasure; if he could survive the pain that the desert could inflict, it seemed, then he would have defeated whatever inner desert it was that compelled him. He was in search of sensation, as if, unsure of his capacity to feel anything at all, he had to seek out the extremes of sensation, of danger, or of pain in order to reassure himself that he was alive. His joy in speeding at night on his motorcycle, a joy that resulted in his death in 1935, was of that nature—a man alone, fighting the elements and, by fighting them, rising above them. He might as well have gone to the South Pole, for what attracted him in the desert was its extremism. The choice of the desert over the extremes of the Antarctic was determined partly by his interest in archaeology, and partly by England's interests in expanding its empire.

Like all the great English adventurers, Lawrence was a product of Oxbridge, the elite college system of Oxford and Cambridge. He spent most of 1910 to 1914 in the Middle East, working under Sir Charles Leonard Woolley in excavations at Carchemish on the Euphrates and spending his free time wandering through the area, learning the language, the customs, and more important still, the politics, establishing contact with the various Arab freedom societies.

Inevitably, he became more the spy than the archaeologist, and may indeed have been so from the outset. While he was in Carchemish, the British army had been involved in intensive surveying activity in southern Palestine, with five surveying teams constantly in the field. Troubled by the German influence in the Ottoman Empire and by the area's strategic sensitivity as a safeguard of access to the Suez Canal, the

British were preparing for a possible war in the Middle East. By 1914, matters were urgent, and Woolley and Lawrence were called down to Beersheba from Carchemish. The Palestine Exploration Fund had requested them on loan from the British Museum for a short but intense survey of the Negev and the northern Sinai, a survey ordered by Lord Kitchener for military reasons, yet run by the Palestine Exploration Fund to give it an archaeological guise. Woolley was the true archaeologist; Lawrence, the military-intelligence man. In an intensive six-weeks effort, the two mapped out the area. Woolley discovered important new archaeological information, published in *The Wilderness of Zin*, and Lawrence, by dint of his knowledge of the Beduin and their ways, gained access to places to which the Turks had refused permission for military reasons. The maps were published only after World War I.

At the outbreak of war, Lawrence was rejected for army service, judged as "physically below fighting standard." He was anemic-looking and only five feet five and one-half inches tall. Nevertheless, he got himself attached to the Geographic Section of the General Staff at Whitehall, transferred to the Military Map Department of the Intelligence Service in Cairo, thence to general intelligence as staff captain at General Headquarters in Cairo, and finally from the Military Intelligence Service to the Arab Bureau, which was under the direct orders of the Foreign Office. Once out of the War Office, he began his career as a soldier in the field, leading the Beduin in their harassment of the Hejaz railway and on to take Damascus.

Yet he never revealed why, thus leaving an enigma for hundreds of scholars to puzzle over. "The strongest motive throughout had been a personal one, not revealed here," he wrote when it was over, "but present to me, I think, every hour of these two years. Active pains and joys might fling up, like towers, among my days: but, refluent as air, this hidden urge re-formed, to be the persisting element of life, till near the end. It was dead, before we reached Damascus." Whatever it was, it died in the vividly described night of sadistic treatment at Deraa, and as far as Lawrence was concerned, only the legend remained. The soul behind it had been broken, and its secret buried. All that remains is speculation about a man trying to prove himself against some inner devil, and about a loyal Briton serving his Empire.

T. E. Lawrence's desert experience took away from him whatever self-respect he had or was striving to attain. It left him a hollow man, but not so hollow that he could not envy and admire Charles Montagu Doughty, who maintained a strong sense of personal integrity throughout his time in the desert. Both men spent two years among the Beduin; but where Lawrence was the honored leader, dressed in the fine robes of a Meccan sheikh, Doughty dressed like and traveled with the poor, earning his keep by the practice of simple medicine. Both went far beyond the point of physical and spiritual exhaustion in the desert; but where Lawrence would trip off to Cairo for rest and recreation, Doughty spent a full two years without hearing so much as a word of English. Doughty's great account *Travels in Arabia Deserta* reveals him as far the more human of the two, a wise and gentle and very patient man who had the great gift of a clear and unfettered perception.

Lawrence recognized this, paying tribute to this fine Englishman in his introduction to a modern version of *Travels in Arabia Deserta*. He described Doughty as "book learned, but simple in the arts of living, ignorant of camels, trustful of every man, very silent." But he paid him what was clearly, for Lawrence, the utmost compliment:

"We export two chief kinds of Englishmen, who in foreign parts divide themselves into two opposed classes. Some feel deeply the influence of the native people, and try to adjust themselves to its atmosphere and spirit. . . . They are like the people but not of the people, and their half-perceptible differences give them a sham influence often greater than their merit. . . . The other class of Englishman is the larger class. In the same circumstances of exile they reinforce their character by memories of the life they have left. . . . They impress the peoples among whom they live by reaction, by giving them an ensample of the complete Englishman, the foreigner intact.

"Doughty is a great member of the second, the cleaner class. . . . His seeing is altogether English, yet at the same time his externals, his manners, his dress, and his speech were Arabic, and nomad Arab, of the desert. The desert inhibits considered judgments; its bareness and openness make its habitants frank. Men in it speak out their minds suddenly and unreservedly. Words in the desert are clear-cut. Doughty felt this contagion of truthfulness sharply. . . ."

Travels in Arabia Deserta is assuredly one of the great travel books in our literature and also one of the finest pieces of anthropology. Yet in it Doughty wrote a humble plea against romanticizing his tale: "As for me who write, I pray that nothing be looked for in this book but the seeing of an hungry man and the telling of a most weary man; for the rest, the sun made me an Arab, but never warped me to Orientalism." Forty years later, no one could have been more sensitive to Doughty's plea than Lawrence. Yet where Lawrence gave way to romanticization, Doughty never did.

"The seeing of an hungry man and the telling of a most weary man . . ." These words have haunted me ever since I first read them. For this was the desert that Doughty saw. Not the camaraderie and cruel pranks, the lovelocks or the glitter of proud eyes immortalized by Lawrence, but the unending battle for survival in a land that made mere survival itself an achievement beyond reckoning. Doughty's life with the Beduin was one of hardship and fear, of terrible thirst and hunger, and of poverty.

Lawrence was right: Doughty was a clean man, a man

without preconceptions or an inner devil to fight, an innocent man who stood faithfully by his beliefs, who never stooped to deception to gain his ends, and who never attempted to hide under the guise of a Moslem, even when his refusal to deny his Christianity placed him on the brink of death. Imagine, then, Lawrence's envy at the purity of such passages as the following: "The traveller [in Arabia] must be himself in men's eyes, a man worthy to live under the bent of God's heaven, and were it without a religion: he is such who has a clean human heart and long-suffering under his bare shirt; it is enough, and though the world be full of harms, he may travel to the ends of the world. Here is a dead land whence, if he die not, he shall bring home nothing but a perpetual weariness in his bones. The Semites are like to a man sitting with a cloaca to his eyes, and whose brows touch heaven. Of the great antique humanity of the Semitic desert, there is a moment in every adventure, wherein a man may find his peace with them, so he know the Arabs."

Doughty was never in "my" desert, in the Sinai and Negev. The desert he knew was the Arabian desert, the vast unexplored land of what is now Saudi Arabia. He was never a spy, though he was often suspected of being one by the Beduin whom he met. And reasons of empire played no part in his wanderlust. He wanted to investigate ancient rock inscriptions, but above all, he wanted to write a book in perfect English. *Travels in Arabia Deserta* was published in 1888, eleven years after Doughty left Arabia, and thereafter he wandered no longer, spending the rest of his life writing epic and dramatic poetry.

Doughty was a romantic. Not a romantic in the sense that Lawrence was, exaggerating or misrepresenting scenes or events in order to sharpen his claims. Nor a romantic in the sense of great tales of adventure, told in order to entrance and suspend disbelief. He was a romantic in that he can still fire the reader with his love of the desert. He loved it both because of and despite itself, a clean, honest love without exaggeration, without adoration, without submission. He told his tale in order that we might feel the desert for what it is and understand the vastness of it. He had no illusions about the desert, and therefore he described its barrenness with unparalleled force: "We look out from every height, upon the Harra, over an iron desolation; what uncouth blackness and lifeless cumber of vulcanic matter!—an hard-set face of nature without a smile for ever, a wilderness of burning and rusty horror of unformed matter. What lonely life would not feel constraint of heart to trespass here! the barren heaven, the nightmare soil! where should he look for comfort?—There is a startled conscience within a man of his *mesquin* being, and profane, in presence of the divine stature of the elemental world!—this lion-like sleep of cosmogonic forces, in which is swallowed up the gnat of the soul within him,—that short motion and parasitical usurpation which is the weak accident of life in matter."

Doughty knew the fierce beauty of the desert as he knew its magic. He could describe its changing moods without any self-interest to distort his perception. He had no point to make, just the desert to travel in and to see.

It is in Doughty that I find my England. Parker, Jarvis, and Lawrence showed me their England again in the desert, but I no longer have any personal connection to all that. Of course, I can laugh with Palmer as he falls on his occiput like a cricket ball on Mount Sinai. I can bask in the warm glow of Jarvis's genial paternalism. I can scorn, with Lawrence, the shock of the English when those whom they helped turned around to demand independence. But it seems to me that of them all, and of all those whom I have not mentioned here, it is above all Doughty who knew and loved the desert, loving it for both its harshness and its grandeur, both its physical poverty and its spiritual richness. And therefore, in my past but ever-present Englishness, it is with Doughty that I identify.

Doughty, with his hollow, haunted eyes, his lined fore-head, full beard, and grand Semitic nose, is the kind of Englishman that made an empire; not by warfare nor by administration nor even by exploration, but by those qualities that remain for me "for ever England"—honesty of detail, honesty of perception, and above all, honesty to oneself.

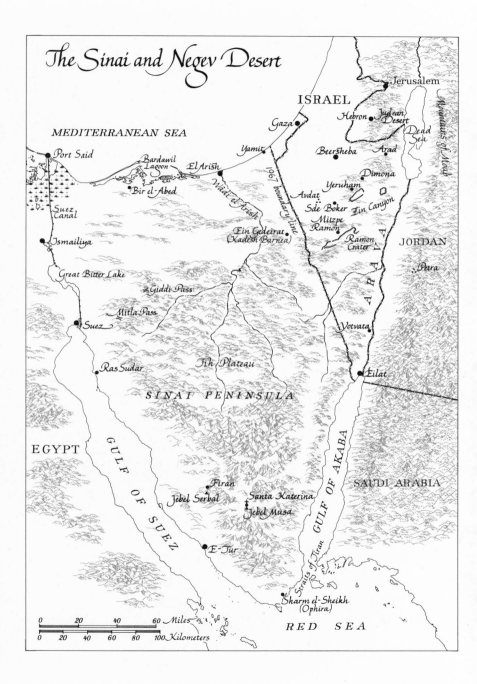

The Sinai and Negev Desert

MEDITERRANEAN SEA

ISRAEL

Jerusalem

Gaza

Hebron
Judean
Desert

Dead
Sea

Yamit

Beersheba
Arad

Port Said

Bardawil
Lagoon
El Arish

Dimona

Bir el-Abed

Yeruham

Avdat
Sde Boker
Ein Canyon

Wadi el Arish

Suez
Canal

Ein Gedeirat
(Kadesh Barnea)

Mitzpe
Ramon

1967 boundary line

Ismailiya

Ramon
Crater

JORDAN

Petra

Great Bitter Lake

Giddi Pass

Mitla Pass

ARAVA

Suez

Yotvata

Ras Sudar

Tih Plateau

Eilat

SINAI PENINSULA

Mountains of Moab

EGYPT

GULF OF SUEZ

GULF OF AKABA

SAUDI ARABIA

Firan
Jebel Serbal

Santa Katerina
Jebel Musa

E-Tur

Straits of Tiran

Sharm el-Sheikh
(Ophira)

RED SEA

0   20   40   60 Miles
0   20   40   60   80   100 Kilometers

PART ONE

THE DESERT ITSELF

1 · Mountains

I have never seen such ugly mountains as those of Santa Katerina, watershed of the red granite peaks of the southern Sinai. Even now that I know and love the area, I feel as I did when I gazed on it for the first time: if I were just to touch any one of those jagged peaks, it would draw blood. My heart caught with the heaviness of doubt and disappointment; where I had expected majesty, I saw only a bleak deformity.

That first time was in a midsummer heat wave, with the temperatures close to 115 degrees. It was arduous and unpleasant driving as we struggled through the narrow Wadi Saal, the heat exacerbating our sense of claustrophobia. The soft grace of the sandstone formations in the mountains nearer to the coast, wind-worked into the forms of intricate jewelry or Gaudí architecture, was eroded from memory by the hard gray granite of the Saal Canyon, by the relentless grind of gravel on tires, and by the constant grating of sharp rocks on the chassis. And when we finally emerged from the Saal to be confronted by that giant triangle of red granite peaks—the gaunt, harsh goal of our journey—it seemed that all my misgivings were well-founded.

Anyone going to Santa Katerina hears too much about the place. Perhaps too many people have been there. There are those who have been there for the day, in and out by plane or command car to climb Mount Sinai and then rush on to the next stop on the tour. There are those who have become "Santa freaks," who have been there a few times and whose eyes go misty with a special light as they murmur a knowing

"Ah, Santa," implying that anyone who has not been there is somehow a lesser kind of person, ignorant of an experience incomparable in scope and depth. And then there are those who tuck Santa away within their souls as a place apart to serve their spiritual need for humility, safe in the knowledge that this humility does not have to be acted upon. "You must go to Santa to know the desert," they say, "to realize the grand indifference of nature to man, a sense of your place in the universe."

Though Santa is many things for many people, nearly all use two particular words to describe it: *beautiful* and *awe-inspiring*. But long before I set foot in those mountains, something in me rebelled against these words. They were too easy, too convenient. They told me nothing about this mountain desert, yet I could feel them insidiously working their way into my mind, preparing me to experience beauty and awe above all.

No, I would not see beauty, I decided. I would try to see beyond beauty, to see what it was that so overwhelmed people that they fell back on this poor overused word for something that had to be far greater. And I was as stubborn about awe. *Awe*, like *beauty*, seemed to block vision, preventing the eyes, minds, and hearts of those who use it from experiencing directly the basis of that awe. Perhaps *awe* prevents understanding by protecting us against it. For the basis of awe is surely fear, and none of us like to admit fear.

Even so, I did not expect to find these mountains ugly. There was no grace at all to them. It was as though some huge person, his hands spilling over with a scalding mass of volcanic and metamorphic rock, had let it fall all together to the ground. Thinking only of saving his hands and salving the pain in them, he had cared nothing for how it would look. Heedless of the jumble of peaks and crags on the ground, he had abandoned them and retreated in silence to lick his wounds.

I spent the first couple of days in the area scrambling and

climbing over the rocks, trying to avoid using my hands because the hard, rough granite can indeed draw blood. And I found that my body changed my relationship to the environment. The eye became only one mode of relating to the mountains; when I began walking, my hands, feet, and whole body joined in to create a new exhilaration: by moving over and through the mountains, I became, in a sense, part of them. Because the granite is so rough, I found that I could run up rock faces, my soft desert boots grasping the surface easily, so that all I had to do was maintain momentum. Of course I was eventually to sprain a tendon running up and down these rocks, since I have never come to terms with my mountain-goat fantasy. In the Negev sometimes I watch the ibex and try to follow the paths they take; inevitably, I get stuck halfway down a cliffside in sudden frightened awareness that I am not a mountain goat. But I have only to see another rock face for the fantasy to reoccur. No amount of sprains and frights can discourage it.

The mountains thus became accessible, however inhuman they seemed from afar. Being on them and in them changed them for me. It made them no less ugly. But a whole world of peaks and ravines was there to be explored and played on, walked over and sat on, dreamed and meditated on. Gradually, they entered a realm beyond aesthetics, as though I were getting to know someone I was beginning to love—no longer passing judgment, but simply finding out more and more.

Then, however unwillingly at first, I began to admit that it is indeed a wonderful feeling to sit and see mountains falling away from you on all sides, ridge after ridge like frozen waves of a sea—this land that was once called Arabia Petraea, "Petrified Arabia." But still I felt no humility, nor any wonder at the grandeur of God's works and the smallness of human beings. I enjoyed the mountains but was not awed by them; perhaps I was too busy playing the mountain goat.

Only later did I realize that I was avoiding Mount Sinai itself those first few days. Avoiding it, yet always aware of that strange square-mile block of red granite bounded by deep ravines, its highest peak thrusting up, black and volcanic, at its southernmost point. It has many names, this mountain. In English, it is known simply as Mount Sinai, or the Holy Mountain. In Hebrew, they call it Har Moshe, "Moses' Mountain," and in deference to it, call the whole range around it Har HaGavoha, "High Mountain." In Arabic, it has no single name, but is divided into two—one name, Jebel Safsafa, "Willow Peak," for the vast block of red granite, and another, Jebel Musa, "Moses' Peak," for the holy peak itself. These are the names given and used by the Beduin, who live in the area and therefore differentiate far more carefully than outsiders between places and peaks. Because the Beduin names are the most exact, these are the ones that I use. But of all the mountain's names, I love most that given by Nikos Kazantzakis in his book *Journeyings:* "The God-trodden mountain."

In those days, though, I was not ready for Kazantzakis's passionate mysticism. Left to my own devices, I would have snorted at the idea of the God-trodden mountain and set off by camel for the most difficult peaks in the area, eager to ignore sprains and aches for the pleasure of playing mountain goat once again. But my stubborn refusal to acknowledge the beauty that most people saw in the High Mountain had intrigued the area's chief archaeologist, Avner Goren. He invited me to join a small group of field-station guides whom he was taking up to the Safsafa the next day. Maybe, he said, then I would see. Though he spoke softly and quietly, it was a challenge. Perhaps it was a challenge because it was put exactly that way, without the anger or resentment that most Santa people expressed when they heard me say how I felt. And so I was to tread the God-trodden mountain.

For fifteen hours, until well after sunset, we walked, scrambled, ran over, sat on, and went into nearly every peak, ravine, cave, and valley on the Safsafa. And I began to feel the magic of this mountain.

The highest peak of Mount Sinai, Jebel Musa, is hidden. You may glimpse it from certain of the mountains round about, but as you approach from the ravines below, you see only the massive soaring walls of the Safsafa, with no hint at what is above. Whichever of the five ancient routes you take up those walls, you see not a glimpse of Jebel Musa and the tiny chapel atop it until you stand on the Safsafa itself—and then only from certain places. It is a spiritual preparation and a spiritual shock; only those who are determined to make it this far up the mountain, to the broad expanse of the Safsafa, are privileged even to see the holy peak itself.

Whichever way you come up, the ascent holds surprises: from the east, the three gates on the way up from the Santa Katerina Monastery, a steep ascent through a narrow ravine in which a monk once built, stone by huge stone, thirty-one hundred steps up to the peak; as one ascends from the northwest, the series of small rough-hewn open chapels, no more than semicircles of stone pointing in the direction of the summit, each placed at one of those rare points where you can see the summit; after you have come up from the southwest along the ancient Byzantine way from the abandoned Dir-el-Arbain Monastery, the sudden greened descent alongside the base of Jebel Musa itself, still invisible. All these ways lead abruptly into a large green hollow at the very center of the Safsafa. The Beduin call such a high-mountain hollow a *farsh*. This one, majestic in its suddenness, is called Farsh Eliahu, "Elijah's Farsh," for it was here, they say, that Elijah lived during his forty days and nights on the mountain. From here you can see Jebel Musa, the holy peak. And from here there is only one route up to that peak.

This is the very heart of the mountain. Musa is the eyes, the mind, the soul of Mount Sinai, but Eliahu is the heart. The whole of it is closed around with peaks, as though the mountain were purposely hiding its secret, closing in on itself to protect its magic from the world outside. It seems a very crafty, clever mountain, concealing everything until you are actually standing on it. Only then do you realize that there is a whole world up here, a "secret garden" of peaks and farshes, of greenery and smooth rock faces, of chapels and hermits' caves.

In keeping with this mystic topography, there was once a monk, Stephanos, who would sit at the middle gate on the steps up from the Santa Katerina Monastery, just before the spot where the ravine breaks into Farsh Eliahu, taking confessions from ascending pilgrims. That was in the sixth century. Those he found wanting in spiritual purity he would send back down again, for this self-appointed gatekeeper of the holy mountain knew that only those who are pure can ascend to God's mountain, while those who are impure would be killed by the confrontation. The archway built to shade him as he sat, year after year, is still there. Later, I would yearn for a latter-day Stephanos, one who would allow onto the mountain only those who would ensure its purity, preserve its magic.

It is as though some wise old architect with twinkling eyes had built this mountain in order to create a spiritual tension, a mystic state of anticipation and sudden shock as the sternly forbidding exterior opens up to the pilgrim only after great exertion, suddenly welcoming him into a world of softness and greenery. At the very center of Farsh Eliahu, there is even a well for the weary pilgrim.

By the well stands the strangest cypress tree in the world, its grace and height centering the eye. The tree seems to have grown three times, each time putting forth more greenery; between the spurts of foliage, there is only bare trunk. The green starts and stops, starts and stops, starts and stops—three trees in one, three separate spurts of growth on one and the same trunk. A trinity tree, perhaps. Around this strange tree are other smaller cypresses and a crab-apple tree. From it, the Safsafa fans out in all directions to smaller farshes once tended by hermits, now only grazed by an occasional flock of black goats that scramble up the ravines to the surrounding peaks as you come near, following their barefoot Beduin girl shepherds. Toward the northern end of the mountain, where a bluff overlooks the small plain below in the valley, is the osier tree that gives Jebel Safsafa its name—"Willow Peak."

As I explored this richness with Avner, I began to regret that I was not religious, that I could not let all this work on me as it must work on a deeply religious mind. But I did feel myself searching out the more suggestible, receptive parts of my mind, feeling my way into them so that this strange and mysterious topography could work some kind of magic in me. Later in the day, as we sat on one of the smooth peaks near the willow tree, the wind that comes before sunset blowing hard in our faces, Avner told the story of the monk who was praying on the summit some centuries ago, on Jebel Musa, and whose prayer was answered by a roaring echo in the mountains of "Holy! Holy! Holy!"—but only those who had ears to hear could hear it. Avner smiled deeply, his eyes questioning. I smiled back, slowly shaking my head. The mountains would not roar for me, I thought, but I could understand now how they could roar for some, for a very few. It seemed that I could see them roaring, but not hear them; knowing what was happening, yet still not quite part of it.

Then Avner mentioned that Christian and Moslem traditions forbid sleeping on Jebel Musa. A logical tradition, he said, since the summit is a pure volcanic massif that can support no life, while the Safsafa has life—water, shrubs, even trees. But to me there was more than the logic of geology in the ban. The tradition seemed to pronounce "Where God appeared, let no man sleep." And it was then, of course, that I realized that the next night I would sleep on the summit of Mount Sinai. It would be full moon and midsummer's eve—a night that was to take me from the sublime to the ridiculous. And back again.

Since it was a decision that came out of stubbornness, it overrode fear. I had a score to settle with these mountains; I had to resolve this matter of beauty and awe once and for all. And I knew that this score could only be settled by myself, away from others, in the mountains themselves. It was a matter between them and me. Yet I was very afraid. I was convinced that I would not be able to sleep up on that mountain, alone. I was fully prepared to spend the night awake, thinking and watching. It was not the ban on sleeping there that made me afraid; if anything, that only added to a sense of adventure and served as the trigger to something that was in the making in any case. No, it was the general fear of the desert that urged me on. The fear, quite simply, of being alone in a vast, open expanse. Ironically, part of this fear is a fear of people. What if I were found alone by strangers? Would I be safe? Part of it was a fear of desert creatures, of snakes or scorpions. But the major part of it by far was a diffuse existential fear, that unnameable fear that people face in the desert—that same fear that led people to create a single strong god in the desert. It is, in a way, a fear of being stranded; a fear not of being lost, but of being isolated. It is a fear that we all face, every day of our lives, wherever we live, yet rarely acknowledge; a fear that increases, approaching the limit of awareness, when we are in the desert; and a fear that can no longer be avoided when we are alone in the desert. I knew that I would face this, and I was afraid of the confrontation itself. What drove me on was not a strong personal urge to confront my own fear, no deep need to test myself, but the desert itself. I knew somehow that I would never become in any sense part of this desert, of any desert, would never be able to see and feel what the desert is, until I could feel at ease in it by myself. And I was aware, too, that this might never happen.

Now, with the meeting of midsummer's eve, the full moon, and the discovery of this mysterious mountain, now was the time.

The next afternoon, I stuffed food, ten pints of water, and a sleeping bag into a backpack and set off for the summit of

Mount Sinai. I went along the ravine of the abandoned Dir-el Arbain Monastery and then around the back of the mountain, up a track from the southeast that looked deceptively simple but that my lungs soon acknowledged was in fact quite steep. I was very conscious of being alone. After about an hour and a half, I was halfway up. The path twisted up the red granite into the eastern side of the mountain, where all was in shadow. Above, to my left, loomed the black volcanic mass that was Jebel Musa. The path became steeper, and then, to my dismay, I saw that the only way to go on was up a nearly vertical narrow ravine in the rock. Exhausted from hiking upward in the afternoon heat, I staggered up the cut, practically on all fours. Suddenly, the ravine floor became level. I was in a narrow cut in the rock with high black walls on either side, a kind of small canyon high up in the mountain. Relieved to be on level ground, I walked along it slowly. Into a time of pure and simple joy.

As I walked along that narrow canyon, a flush of red light began to fill it, as though I were walking into a world of a deep rose color, a world warm and welcoming. The light increased in intensity as I neared the end of the canyon, a deep flush of red suffusing everything—the walls, the floor, myself. And then as I came to the end, it burst into a brilliant gold. The steep black walls suddenly fell back and I saw the ground, too, falling away beneath my feet to Farsh Eliahu below, with its trees and shrubs and soft, light-washed rocks. Eagles and bustards wheeled in the valley below. A few yards down from where I stood, the path of broad boulder steps leading up to the summit lay waiting for me.

It seemed that the whole scene had been created just to welcome me, who had come into the light after the dark shadow of the ascent. Here was green and gold after the darkness of shadowed granite and black volcanic rock. My heart still full of that beautiful deep red light that had surrounded and suffused me, I laughed and flopped happily to the ground to take in the whole glorious scene, reveling in the knowledge that I was the only person on this whole mountain.

And it is a measure of my awareness of the magic of this mountain that I did not even think of going back into the canyon to investigate that red light. In retrospect, I know it was not an effect of sunset, for that was still at least two hours away. A trick of the light on that particular type and formation of rock is the most probable explanation. But then and there, it seemed to me something to be accepted in simplicity. Radiantly happy at the very experience of it, I sat and enjoyed it fully, in time.

When that time was over, I rose and began the climb up the steps. From that point, I later found out, there were only fifteen hundred steps of the total thirty-one hundred to the summit from the Santa Katerina Monastery. But I didn't count. Each step was different, most of them well over a foot high. The Byzantine monk who devoted all his life to placing rock on rock, boulder on boulder, had sweated in sun and braved wind and cold to build this path, which had me, young and healthy, sweating and panting just from climbing it. I felt humbled and even humiliated. How many pilgrims had climbed these steps, how many monks, how many tourists even, at all times of day? And here I was laboring at them.

I labored on, well past the point that I come to in climbing any mountain where I wonder What the hell am I doing here? Why did I have to climb it at all? Why must I do such things to myself? And then, with no warning at all in the way the steps were constructed, no gradual easing in steepness, no glimpse of a view to show me how high I had come, I suddenly saw the chapel right in front of me—an ugly, squat little building with broken windows and a creaking roof, with a tiny still more dilapidated mosque beside it. I was on the peak. Bastard mountain, I thought. How could it do this with no preparation? I had not seen the peak at all during the climb up. Only the knowledge that it was there had led me up the mountain, and that knowledge had been forgotten completely in the ascent. The abrupt appearance of the hidden peak was a shock. There was no slow gaining the peak for the familiar feeling of "Phew, I did it, here I am," but a sudden instantaneous revelation of height, as though the mind had been plucked out of a morass of detail and placed on another plane, aloft.

The sun was in descent by now, and the colors were deepening from the monotonous brightness of the day, as if the canvas of the landscape had been touched with a varnish, covering the brashness of new color to make it glow with age and subtle hue. Soon the sun would set. I ate, sharing some nuts with three birds who had come to investigate my strange presence at this time of day. They were small and sand colored, each with a yellow tuft on its head echoed by a patch of yellow on its chest. They bounced and chirped a little, snatched a few nuts, and then flew off to reach their nests before nightfall. I watched the last eagle circling below me as the western horizon began to darken with reds and purples. The sky above me became a deeper and deeper blue, as though someone were languorously drawing a heavy veil over it; *a veil of darkness* became no mere phrase, but a slow and beautiful reality.

The full moon, already high in the sky, had changed from pale white to bright silver, its light rivaling that of the sinking sun until there were two pale suns in the sky. And as the light of east and west balanced and shifted, the mountains seemed to fall into new formations revealed only in this half-light. The double peak of the Safsafa below me now framed the lower triple peak of another more distant summit. I was standing at the top of a giant mountain altar. It rose gradually, majestically, over many miles, flowing upward in a straight line from the multiple crests of distant low ridges to the framed triple peak, up and higher to the double peak, and then up to the apex of the altar—to the single peak of Jebel Musa and myself, standing upright, atop this single peak. Suffused with the sheer physical logic of this being the holy mountain, the metaphysical logic of mysticism, I felt that never had I stood higher than this, that there could be no higher place in the world.

The colors of sunset darkened still more. I lay down again, entranced by the quiet, the hues, the serenity. And it was only after a slight tremor inside me when the sun finally disappeared from sight that I realized that I no longer felt any trepidation. The fear that I had come here to face and to test had been left behind. It had been a fear anticipated in "civilization," a product of another world that had no place in this utter peacefulness.

As dark fell, one lone bird raced across the sky to its nest. Happily, calmly, I lay back on the rock in my sleeping bag—and fell asleep even before the last colors of sunset had left the sky, a deep refreshing sleep from which I awoke from time to time when a brief cold wind touched my face. I would gaze around in calm and content, seeing the huge silver moon above me and the strong shadows it cast on these mountains below, and then close my eyes into sleep again until sometime before dawn.

It may have been a subtle change in the quality of the light that roused me, or a lone bird that sensed something I could not and woke to sing a few forlorn notes. It was still dark. Lying on the smooth high rock to the northeast of the chapel, I was facing north. The moonlight from my left cast strong shadows still; the frozen waves of mountains spreading out around me were still caught in silvered relief. To my right was the vaguest suggestion of the beginnings of another light. At first, it seemed only my imagination, the force of suggestion in my knowing that this other light would come. But gradually the east began to cast its own undeniable light, cold and silvery like that of the moon in the west. As I lay on my back looking up, I saw the whole circle of the sky with myself at the center, as if this were a celestial fish tank and I, the fish, were peering up from the bottom of it. The center of the circle was a deep blue, almost black, dotted with pale stars. Around the

whole of the circle's edge a pale rim enclosed the deepness as
the sun and the moon simultaneously shed their light to create
not east and west, but a perfect halo of lightening sky around
the horizon. The halo faded. The light from the east spread
out farther into the sky; the light in the west retreated,
dimming as the moon began to descend more rapidly.

I saw again the altar of mountains leading up to me as each
level in turn was caught by the shifting lights of rising and
setting spheres. The light in the east became sharper now, and
with it, a dull crimson haze spread around the horizon. As the
red spread and brightened, approaching orange, the moon
sank. It became a deeper and deeper yellow as it descended,
lucent still as it had been all night, but with a less forceful,
mellower hue. When it reached a point just above the
mountaintops to the west, it turned deep gold and then a
golden brown . . . and within the space of a minute it was
gone, blended with the mountains, brown into brown.

I turned eagerly to the east, thinking that the orb of the sun
would rise just as the moon had set, forgetting for a moment
the difference in horizons, the close mountains in the west and
the distant ones in the east. In the open mountainless desert it
can happen—a perfect balance of celestial light with sun and
moon rising and setting in unison. But here, this night, the
sun was not to rise yet, though its light was searching out the
mountain ridges. One by one, their shapes stood out in the
light whose source was still hidden, revealing dimension after
dimension of depth. . . .

Footsteps on the path up. Three young people appeared
carrying cameras and a jerrycan of water. Within a few
minutes there came two more. And then more, until the full
group of thirty-five European tourists straggled up to the
summit. They chattered and huffed after the climb up. A
couple said a tentative good-morning to the sleeping-bag-
swathed figure standing there, just the eyes glaring out
malevolently from the full-length shawl of khaki padding.

They got a gruff grunt in reply. Thereafter I was ignored, but also given as wide a berth as thirty-five people could give me on the narrow confines of that peak.

My resentment of this invasion was rooted in possessiveness. How dare they? I thought. How dare they come up onto *my* mountain?—for it felt that by sleeping there I had made the place mine, linked myself to it in a way that far surpassed the transience of "coming up to look."

All the tourists had cameras slung around them. Giggling and chattering still, they clambered onto the east side of the rock. Cocktail hour on Mount Sinai, I thought grimly. Some sat with camera balanced on knee. Others lay dramatically on their bellies, their cameras in front of their faces like square black projections of their heads. Still others fiddled with lenses and focusing. None looked about them. Once distance and aperture were set, the noise level decreased as they sat, stood, or lay in wait, eyes glued to viewfinders, for what they had come to see. For a moment I wondered what would happen if the sun did not rise, how they would complain, and to whom? It was more than a mischievous passing thought. Although I knew that the sun was going to rise, it now seemed to me a wonder of light and life and color that could not be taken for granted, *must* not if our senses are to remain alive.

As I pondered the possibility of the sun not rising, it began to rise.

The upper rim of that deep red orb appeared slowly over the horizon, lifting with the slow pace of immense power. As it did so, a deep red ring, that same deep red, appeared all around the horizon, as if the sun were about to rise in every direction at once. As I circled around on the rock, the sun and its power surrounded me, and a mass click of shutters welcomed it. Here were human beings worshiping the sun, modern man determined to catch it and frame it. What poor limited children of those fierce ancestors who had no scientific explanations but knew instead fear and wonder, those powerful figures of yore and lore who lived in and respected the desert. Once, it seemed, we knew of better ways to greet that ball of red as it climbed upward above the horizon. Now, there were just the repeated chords of camera shutters clicking, a puny orchestra of technology and the limited views imposed by it.

Then as the cameras did their work, just as the whole orb of the sun gained the horizon, three birds came flying from the Safsafa toward Jebel Musa, three small birds flying fast. And nothing will ever persuade me from the unabashedly romantic and somehow mystic conviction that these three birds were the same three that had visited me before sunset on this same peak. Now they came again in the sunrise, flying straight toward me. Just before they reached the peak, they split dramatically, one veering off to the right, to the east and the risen sun, and two to the left, westward. It was a flight of pure beauty in that many-hued light of sunrise. And it seemed, a flight only for me. For only I saw it; only I was not peering through a camera lens. An omen, I thought. Surely an omen. But of what? I didn't know. I only knew that the meaning of an omen depends on the seer. And I saw too how easy it would be for the slightest occurrence to take on the magical and mystical aspects of an omen. Here, after sunset and sunup, standing on this altar of mountains in the cold strong wind of dawn, there was magic in the air. I could feel the magic, but knew it not. I knew the birds for an omen, but couldn't feel what it would be. "And only those with ears to hear can hear it," said the monk. Only those with eyes to see, also.

The wind blew still colder as the light filled the sky. It must have been the start of this cold wind that woke me before dawn. The women in the tourist group complained of the cold and began photographing each other. They were impervious to the red glow of the Safsafa below them, soon to dissolve into a cold yellow in the early light. Their eyes did not see "God's fingers," the rays of sunlight now beginning to shine strongly through the gaps in the mountain peaks, rays of silvery gold dust reaching for millions of miles through mountains to valleys, through space to earth. One of these rays touched this peak, and facing it, I closed my eyes in its pale light.

The tourists had not the patience to sit and watch the different peaks light up in turn as the rays of sunlight touched them, pointing out their heights one by one in descending order. Many of them were still looking east, wondering why the show had been so brief, unaware that although they had seen the sun rising, they had completely missed the sunrise. And so they began leaving, some thirty minutes after they had arrived on the summit. They filed down below the rock on which I stood, chattering still, until first their figures and then their voices completely disappeared.

Happy to be alone again on my mountain, I sat vainly hoping that the sun would warm me a little and watched the jagged lines of mountains adjust to the daylight. I had breakfast, perched there on the rock: crackers and cheese, dates and nuts, an apple and water. In that chill early light, as everything shifted from night to day, I realized that this is indeed a magic mountain, beyond all questions of beauty and ugliness. Now I could understand why this should be the holy mountain, this and no other, no matter who chose it as such—Moses, God, Byzantine monks, hermits, followers of pre-Christian cults. It does not matter, for the mountain holds the magic within its form. It is a mountain conceived for mysticism, for those who have ears to hear and eyes to see.

The sun rose, and daytime assumed its undisputed place. I began to feel restless. In the cold light, this no longer felt like "my mountain." Puzzled at this feeling but accepting it for the time being, I began my slow descent, resting and drinking water down below the summit in Farsh Eliahu, lying on the rocks there to warm myself before descending the steps past Stephanos's gate to the monastery below.

In the forecourt of the monastery, I sat propped against a birch tree, writing in a tiny notebook as I waited for the companions I had arranged to meet there. The Beduins in the forecourt kept a respectful distance when they saw me writing so busily; sitting quietly on a stone bench by the monastery wall, they waited for nine o'clock, when the monks would open the tiny door into the monastery itself. The place was cool and peaceful. The sun dappled through the birch leaves; a slight breeze stirred them into a whisper. Sometimes as I wrote, I would stop and look up and around me, blinking, and sing a little, quietly—a Hebrew folksong whose words I don't even know. And with that song still in my head, I would write again of my night on the mountain.

Only some months later, however, was I to find the words for that night's feeling of belonging to the mountain, and the mountain to me. They were the words of Laurens van der Post in his novel *A Far-Off Place*, explaining in Bushman terms why these desert nomads name the places where they sleep when traveling through the Kalahari: "So that the place should know that they were feeling how the place had given itself to them and how they in turn were giving something of themselves to the place . . . [so that] the place can always feel that although they themselves have gone, they have left feeling that something utterly of themselves would always be there feeling itself part of it."

An "Amen" to such places.

2 · Fear

Whenever I walk into the desert alone, I look back every now and again at the buildings from which I set out or at my car parked forlornly at the foot of a ravine. I say to myself that I look back to see how far I have come or to get my bearings, and I resolutely set aside the comfort I derive from still seeing the signs of human civilization. After all, my aim is to get away from all that. But then comes the time when I look back and can no longer see the buildings or the car. Suddenly, there is no sign of human life. And at that moment, I feel my heart beating stronger, the blood pulsing through me. There is a heightened awareness that I am alone, out of reach of other humans—the only thinking, sentient creature in this vast landscape. It is an exhilarating feeling, and terrifying too. For this heightened sense of vitality comes together with the awareness of death and its possibilities. As I stand alone amid all the rock and sand, stone and gravel, my body busily proclaims its vitality; but the very contrast between this living, beating, breathing body and the still, silent wilderness in which it stands impels me into recognition of the intricate and unassailable symbiosis of life and death. Each time anew, the desert forces me into this awareness, an assault on my alienation. Never, it seems, am I so vitally, healthily aware of being alive.

Many people tend to equate the desert with a lack of life. In a supreme leap of egocentric imagination, they see lack of life as human death and feel their vitality shriveling as they look on its face. But there are others who thrive on the paradox of life in the midst of utter stillness, and they search out the desert for this reason. Indeed, it seems to me that all Western society's dealings with the desert—exploration, development, religious experience—are rooted in the image of the desert as a deathly place, and that the fascination with the desert is part of the ageless human struggle to come to terms with the conditions of existence, with the inevitability of death after life and the search for life within life.

We tend to see ourselves as reflected in the eyes of others, and sometimes we come to depend on them to such an extent that we lose our own private sense of being, seeking reassurance from others of the very fact that we are alive. And where that reassurance does not exist, as in the desert, we become afraid—not of the desert itself, but of what we see as its emptiness, as though that emptiness would slowly penetrate our souls and drain the life force from us. We create an easy progression of images for the desert—empty, void, forsaken, deserted. And we fear the image we have created, for in that image, we see our own.

It seems to me that it is not physical death we fear in the desert so much as death of the soul. We fear that we will be swamped by these vast expanses and thus lose our sense of self, the ego that is the basis of our relation to the world. We fight this battle for "self" every day of our lives, though we are barely aware of it. But the desert brings the battle to the forefront of our consciousness, where we cannot ignore it. And therefore we tend to resent and fear the desert. We can no longer hide behind busyness and other people. In the desert, we are truly alone, face to face with ourselves—and many of us shrink from the emptiness we fear to find within, the mirror of the emptiness we project onto the desert itself.

There are some few people who are drawn to face this fear. By going forward to meet this fear in the desert, they find themselves the greater for it. It is as though they were standing at the very front line of life, looking over the ravines, plains, and mountains of death. By facing the emptiness of the desert, they find the fullness in themselves. T. E. Lawrence was such a man—a complex misfit in his own society, who felt truly alive only when in the desert, searching in vain for the peace of mind that C. M. Doughty had found there a generation before. Both men revealed what lured them to the desert only in passing hints and phrases. Their reluctance to enter into this in writing is understandable, for feelings and emotions were not the open book in the literature of fifty or a hundred years ago that they are today. Even today, though, there remains one feeling that is still largely closed to expression, and that is fear. For the fear of being afraid is stronger even than the fear of death. It is, perhaps, the strongest fear of all.

The longer I was in the desert, the more I realized that I was both fascinated by it and fearful of it and that this combination of fascination and fear was an irresistible lure. But when I tried to explore this feeling with others, I found that they denied it forcefully. Too forcefully, it seemed to me. Worse, they resented me for mentioning it and queried my motivation with an accusatory tone. Thus it was with immense relief and gratitude that I discovered *The Fearful Void*, an account by the English journalist Geoffrey Moorhouse of his attempt to cross the Sahara from east to west in 1972. He was to end his journey halfway to his goal in exhaustion and illness. But he told it with great courage and honesty. Seeing the Sahara for the first time from the air, he wrote that "my emotions produced two responses in quick succession. First there was an almost sensuous thrill of anticipation; impulsively, I wanted to grapple with the void down there, I wanted to plunge into it, I wanted to stretch myself out to its limits. Instantly, my heart and my body recoiled from the prospect. . . . I did not need to look far for a justification of this journey. It was there in my instant recoil from the prospect of commitment, in the fearful sweat that sprang out of my palms. I would use this journey to examine the basis of my fear."

Moorhouse discovered that it was not fear of the desert, but the diffuse fear of life itself that led him on. This fear is something much less spectacular and far more commonplace in most people's experience, he wrote, than we are willing to admit or even able to identify. Yet it severely circumscribes the scope of our lives. And "while there can be no solution so facile as that expressed by 'learning to conquer fear,' it is possible to come to terms with it, to grow stronger and straighter through the encounter with it."

There is something extraordinarily clean about this fear as it is experienced in the desert. This is partly because the desert itself is clean. No matter how much dust, sand, and sweat I have collected on my body and clothes in the desert, I have never felt dirty or grimy. I have slept on the ground of the desert and eaten food that has fallen on that ground, in the knowledge that it is clean—a world unto itself, unsullied by human activity. But the cleanness is more than physical. Fear in the desert is uncomplicated by other people. It is stripped bare of the anxieties and hopes that accompany fear in social and political situations. When we fear other people's opinions of ourselves, we are demeaned by that fear, feeling ourselves the lesser for it. But there is nothing demeaning about the fear of the desert. It has the cleanness of direct confrontation. Here, we encounter very private yet universal basics—the elemental fear of the experience of ourselves as alive, and the accompanying awareness of death. This fear never entirely disappears, but awareness of it and confrontation with it heightens our understanding, warmth, intelligence, and pleasure in the very experience of living. The clarity of the desert itself enters the soul, blasting away the involvements of urban life as the wind-flung sand blasts the rock into smooth austerity. The desert can take us beyond what we think of as ourselves into another wider order of being where the sense of self is irrelevant. It is a world beyond ourselves, an infinity of time and space that offers a directness of vision, an honesty, a simplicity of being that would be childlike were it all not suffused with the adult wonder that this is even possible.

But the desert does not grant such experience easily. Its harshness includes very real dangers—snake or spider bite and scorpion sting, dehydration, fall, injury. The greatest danger, as people experience it, is that of being lost in the desert. It is associated with the fear of a thirsty, desperate, isolated death, of being swallowed up forever in this vastness, one's bones picked clean by predators or covered by the inexorable sands. . . . This fear, I think, reflects a deeper sense of loss, a lack of faith in ourselves and in the validity of our very existence. It is the fear not only of being out of our physical element, but also of being beyond our limited human dimensions of time and space. The more afraid we are, the smaller and more insignificant we feel, and the less faith we have in ourselves. This is surely the basis of the awe so many people feel in the desert and of the great monotheistic religions that grew out of this awe. Within this vast emptiness of desert, an ancient people felt a need to establish a single unifying force that would give meaning to their lives here. The indifference of this vast nature to man could be overridden by the supernatural will of a god in the spirit of the desert: a harsh and willful desert godhead for desert people.

To the Beduin, the desert people whose origins are hidden in history but whose sense of tradition and faith has kept them alive in the desert for centuries, that godhead is Allah, the ultimate source of good and evil. Good is *wusa*—latitude, wide pasturelands, and the freedom to move through the desert to search them out. Evil is *dhig*—constriction, being cut off from the expanses of the surrounding desert. As one Beduin poet in the northwest Sinai put it,

> Oh Allah, according to your order, life is either wide or narrow,
> And if you decree it be wide, there will be no wrong.

The traditional Beduin life-style is based on fear of constriction and restraint and a longing for expanse. The very attributes of the desert that generally so frighten the Western mind—its vastness, its seemingly limitless force—are the Beduin's blessings, an integral part of Beduin life and values and religious beliefs. The modern Westerner often fears what the traditional Beduin longs for. For while our civilization centers on ourselves, the Beduin's focuses on the environment, on the desert itself. And since the Beduin are the only people to have existed through history continuously in the desert, it seems that this is what the desert demands—a deep commitment to its own imperative and a sloughing off of our intense self-centeredness.

But if so, then the desert is basically antisocial in Western terms. It militates against the basic values of Western life. Where the Westerner strives for control of his environment, placing himself at the center of the universe he would rule, the Beduin acknowledges the power of the environment over him, its power over human life and death, and his submission to a force far larger than he. In the desert it seems that it could not be any other way, for those who know the desert cannot deceive themselves as to its power.

The Beduin accept this power with a large degree of fatalism—the fatalism that Islam was to adopt from the Beduin beliefs of pre-Islamic days. There is no railing against fate in Beduin life but a simple acceptance of it, with the accepting phrases of condolence in death common to all those societies that Westerners regard as "primitive," phrases such as "Meeting with god is a privilege," or "People always die, people always pass away." When his infant daughter died of a snakebite, for example, a Negev Beduin could still smile as he made up a poem of sad acceptance:

> No matter, for fate visits all one night,
> And the worm will eat each of us with great delight.

Man's existence in the desert is reduced to a cosmic whim. The very line between life and death so essential to Western

philosophy is blurred, and the Western ambition for control of
the conditions of life is challenged. Inevitably, the Westerner
fears this imperative of the desert. Unsure of the basis of his
own life, he shrinks from the challenge of the desert, afraid
that he too will succumb to the fatalism of the Beduin.

As Western society slowly spreads into the desert, its
representatives seek to armor themselves against this challenge. The Israelis found their armor by developing an
ambitious ideology of conquering the desert. They coined the
term "Making the desert bloom," the cornerstone of an
ideology that afforded them some protection against the
desert's evident hostility to the idea of a settled population. It
also became a means of protecting the values of the basically
Western Israeli society—of guarding against the antisocial pull
of the desert, its wildness and unpredictability. The desert
would not leave its imprint on the Israelis who went into it;
they would leave their imprint on the desert. In the United
States, the armor against the desert's challenge was not
ideology but technology and the familiar fripperies of the
American culture. Casinos and nightclubs have been erected
in the middle of the American desert as though it were a giant
child's sandbox. And in more direct expression of the fear of
the desert, the military has reduced to atomic waste what was
perceived in any case as wasteland. Yet within the values of
Western society, the lengths to which man will go to ignore
the imperative of the desert may be justified. For the desert's
challenge to those values—the wild pull toward that ephemeral line between life and death—can be seductively dangerous.
The desert does not always express its power over human life
violently. It can also do so with enticing gentleness.

One night, as I was driving through the Judean Desert, I
was nearly killed by this soft power. I was on the long
winding road down through the Hebron Mountains into the
deep chasm of the Great Rift Valley. It was two in the
morning, and not another car was on the road; there was utter
stillness except for the purr of the motor as I let the car coast

downward. Through the gaps in the mountains, I saw the Dead Sea glittering below me. Over on the other side of the Rift Valley the naked mountains of Moab rose majestically, large and near in the light of the full moon rising above them. It was as though someone far above this vast barren landscape had shaken silver dust over it, and the dust, restless, now rose off the ground in a luminous mist to invade the blackness of night. The air moved warm and silent through my hair, stroking my head as I steered around the hairpin bends and glimpsed through the heights and depths of mountains the silvery lake lying below, the lowest lake in the world. The full, round ball of the moon, huge in its rising, shone over the desert as though it were its own, as though without the moon, the landscape, and I too, would cease to exist, would disappear into the nothingness of night. I came out of a bend facing directly into the moon, and it seemed that the moon was beckoning to me, drawing me forward into its circle of grace and light, straight forward. . . . I turned the wheel abruptly, tires screeching, skidding violently as I just caught the next hairpin bend. But as I came out of it, there was the moon again, still beckoning, still inviting. . . . If I were just to set the wheel straight, I felt, the car would lift off this descent through the mountains and fly ahead into that shining sphere of beauty. A part of me knew that if I did so, the car would careen off the road into one of the ravines below. But another part of me was entranced, entering into a spell woven of moon and warm air, of silence and shimmering light. And at each bend, the rational part of me had to work harder to assert its will and to turn the wheel, to keep the body alive where the soul was longing to soar over this deep gouge in the earth's crust and meet the moon. So that it was with the most extraordinary mixture of relief and disappointment that I finally drove out of those mountains into the level stretch at the bottom of the Rift Valley, the moon now high above me, that great salt lake shimmering by my side, and myself, earthbound, driving northward toward Jerusalem.

That time I was alone. But there was another time, in the mountains of the southern Sinai, when I was with friends. Starting out at four in the morning, we climbed up the jagged granite peaks and down into the deep ravines that separated them. All morning, I played the mountain goat, dashing up and down, happily running over rock faces. I used up far more energy than my two slow but sure companions, and far more of the water in my body. Yet obstinately, I only drank when they drank, and I paid no heed when each time one of them stopped to urinate, I felt no need to do so. I wanted just to climb on and on, to run and leap over these gaunt mountains. By near midday, we had stretched out into a line, myself in the lead and my friends strung out fifty and a hundred yards behind me. We were in a long, wide, curving valley filled with intricately worked boulders, the kind of landscape where Henry Moore would have thrown up his hands in despair and ceased working forever. And as with one of his sculptures, I had to touch and feel each boulder, climb up onto and through them and wander back and forth across the valley to see them from all angles, feeling the pleasure in my hands and underfoot of rock worked smooth by wind.

It was some time before I realized that my friends were far behind me, beyond sight. I crept beneath a huge boulder lying at an angle to the ground, the first shade I had come across since sunrise. Lying there in the coolness of this stone belly, my eyes slit lizardlike against the glare of the sun, I slowly curled my tongue around my mouth to feel the damp of it. It occurred to me that I should drink, but the water was in my backpack, and I was too lazy to reach for it. When my friends caught up, I crawled out to greet them, and found my voice deep and slow, slightly slurred. Shortly afterward, I stumbled for the first time, on a large flat smooth boulder where there was nothing to stumble over but my own feet. My companions urged me to drink, but I refused. I was no longer at all thirsty. But then I stumbled again. When we reached a point where three boulders had fallen into the valley to create a tunnel of shade beneath them, I no longer wanted to walk. I tried to persuade my companions to go ahead; I'd follow them in a short while, I said, I just wanted to rest a little. But I knew what it was that I wanted—to lie down in that seductive shade and close my eyes, knowing that if I did so, I would never open them again. I wanted to surrender to a gentle darkness within me; not to talk nor walk nor drink, just to give way to this beautiful languor in my limbs and eyes, to be left here in peace. But my friends would not let me. The slow slurred speech, the stumbling, the refusal to drink, the fact that I had not urinated for hours—they knew the signs of dehydration, as did I, though I refused to acknowledge them now. Gradually they persuaded me to take a sip of water, an orange, some nuts, more water . . . and after a while, though I still wanted only to sleep, they judged that I could now go on. They kept me carefully between them as the valley got narrower and deeper until we reached water—a small pool in the rocks. We stripped and lay immersed for half an hour or so, until my body began to cool. And then I drank. My eyes and mouth cleared; I no longer wanted to sleep. But it was not until much later that day, as we lay around the fire in the evening, that I suddenly turned around in my sleeping bag and thanked them. I had just realized that if I had been alone that day, I would indeed have lain down to sleep beneath those boulders—and would be there still.

Times such as these have wrought a basic transformation in my fear of the desert. Those first, original fears of space and isolation are still there whenever I set out alone into the desert, and yet I feel almost thankful for them, for through them, I have never felt so sharply alive. But now there is a new, strange fear, a fear not of the desert, but of the readiness within myself to be seduced into dying in it, an innocent yet knowing temptation to flirt with that thin, blurred line between life and death. I try to tell myself that this longing to surrender to the force of the desert is a longing for experience. But I know that in so doing, I would fool only myself. For the force becomes so strong for a moment—and the danger is when that moment trips over into eternity—that I forget that without the body, experience has no meaning. If the body dies, then that moment of oneness with the desert dies with it, reduced to just another pile of bones bleached by the glaring sun, infinity become merely food for jackals and hyenas. The desert cares nothing for my experience of it. It makes of human concepts of life and death a trivial paradox, as though it were toying with godlike carelessness with the strings that circumscribe the movements of human life. So my fear now is based on a deep respect for the desert, and on a recognition of its power to thrust me into that fearful yet exhilarating exploration of my own life and my own death and—within the unheeding desert—the insignificance of both life and death.

3 · Sand

The scorpion is trying to burrow into the sand. It must succeed or die. Though it is only a couple of hours after dawn, it is already very hot, and the sand of the gathering sandstorm stings hard in our faces as we watch. On the thin translucent green skin of the scorpion, that stinging must be torture. A few more minutes of exposure like this and the scorpion will have to die. It tries to burrow again. And again. And yet again. But each time it pushes its head into the sand and frantically works its front and middle legs, the sand shifts in the driving wind, and the beginnings of the burrow collapse.

We watch, attuned to the urgency of the scorpion's plight by the high drumming of the wind in our ears, the heat, the hard massage of sharp grains of sand on our hands and faces. Mesmerized, we see its sting gradually go limp, slowly lower over onto one side, uncurling slightly. The translucence of the green skin begins to dull. Soon the tail is limply curled at the scorpion's side. We have been sitting absolutely still, watching this, for ten minutes.

Now, trying to make the scorpion's task easier, we scrape out deep rifts in the sand for it. But the wind is too strong. For the last time, the creature tries to burrow its way into safety—in vain.

And then, it simply gives up. It just lies there, flat out, and lets the hot flying sand cover it. Within a few seconds, it is competely hidden from sight.

As the wind covers the inert greenness, Udi, our guide, looks up gravely: "Now just imagine if that were one of us, caught out here in the storm with no water, no clothes or shelter against the sand and wind, while it's getting hotter all the time. Just think how we too would look desperately for shelter and then, not finding any . . ."

Despite the sandstorm, we are in a comfortable position from which to consider such a dilemma. We have plenty of water and clothes to protect us. We know where we are—in the inland dunes of Halutsa, which spread from the central Negev westward to the Mediterranean—and we know that we have only a few miles to walk through the dunes and the storm to the nearest road.

These certainties give me the security within which to enjoy the storm. Small certainties they may seem to some, but they are large ones in the desert. The sun has long been invisible. In fact, I can scarcely see the next dune. Blanketed in the state of excited tranquillity that any storm seems to arouse in me, I am simply pleased to be in sand dunes during a sandstorm. Instead of being drained by the battering of sand and wind, my energy is high from the few hours' sleep curled into the sand during the night and the waking to the silvery dawn preceding the storm. My senses are soothed, even numbed maybe, into a smiling haze of acceptance of physical discomfort—an enjoyment of sensory deprivation beyond all but the overpowering elements of swirling sand, stinging wind, the howl of the storm in my ears, and the taste of it in my mouth.

I would love just to stay here sitting in the sand, next to the scorpion's grave. My back is to the wind, and in my hand is a cup of very sweet tea, with sand rapidly collecting in the bottom. Sooner or later the storm will pass, and until it does I would do what the creatures here do, big and small, in their various ways—find my niche, stay put, and wait it out.

If I were here alone, I would be very afraid. But we are a large group of ten, led by Udi and Gabi from the Sde Boker Field Station. And I already know that if I were to be lost in the desert, then I would want to be with Udi when it happened.

In the United States, Udi would be considered short. But in the Middle East, an area where tall people are rare, he is accounted a fair height. His leg muscles are so developed that he looks almost lopsided, for he has a slender torso that seems out of balance atop such powerful legs. He has a splendid head of loosely tousled blond hair and a beard that covers almost all of his face. Seeking the face behind the beard, you see only the small straight nose and the deep gray blue of the eyes. Later in the summer, he'll shave off his beard, revealing a face of surprising beauty, with the clear lines of youthful innocence. But lacking the patience to shave every day he'll let the beard grow again, so that for two months his aura will be one of a sinister slovenliness, and it will be hard to remember that all these—the fine wildness of beard, the radiant innocence of fresh face, and the sinister quality of growth—are Udi.

As we were being driven into the sand dunes earlier in the day, I'd seen what one can do with muscles such as Udi's. He was sitting next to the driver in the jeep, and I was directly behind him. Suddenly, Udi was no longer in his seat. He hadn't fallen out, and I hadn't noticed him move; he was simply no longer there. The jeep was traveling about twenty miles an hour. I swiveled around to see Udi leaping on all fours across the sand in tremendous bounds, like a cross between a panther and a frog. On the third leap, he came to rest. Then rising with his hands cupped, he came over to the halted jeep to show us the sand lizard he'd caught, mottled gold and brown, sand colors. As amazed by the power of the leaps as by the fact that he'd even spotted the lizard, I asked him how he managed to jump like that. "I really don't know," he replied, looking somewhat surprised. "I don't usually do that; usually I catch them first time." The look in his eyes betrayed the mischief in saying such a thing for effect. But it quickly became evident that it was also a statement of fact.

Gabi, taller and leaner than Udi, is clean-shaven with closely cropped hair. Like Udi, his closest friend, he loves animals and can handle them soothingly and without fear.

Both are in their late twenties. But unlike Udi, Gabi prefers nature to people, music to books, and silence to ideas. He is not a guide and does not want to be, since the job involves working with people, and Gabi has little patience for them. He is the factotum of the field station, and on field trips he jealously guards to himself the tasks of setting up camp and cooking. More practical than Udi, he does what interests him, picks up and assimilates information that he wants and sleeps through the rest, secure in the feeling that here is his place and his work and he will neither leave it nor need more.

Gabi talks little, but things happen to him in the desert. In much the same way that luck seems to happen to those who are ready for it, so do "events" in the desert. Once, he found a fawn with a broken leg in Ein Akev ("Well of the Heel"), some miles away from Sde Boker. He picked it up and carried it back to the field station, then drove into Beersheba with it, where Reuven Yagil, the veterinarian who is also "the camel doctor" for the Israeli army's camel corps, set the leg in plaster. A couple of weeks later, Gabi had to take the fawn into town again to get the plaster taken off. I went with him. We put the fawn in a plastic crate lined with straw, covered it with a piece of tarpaulin, and carefully placed it in the back of the jeep. In Beersheba, we stopped to pick up a few things and foolishly left the jeep unattended for five minutes. The other, human, desert asserted itself. On returning, we found the tarpaulin torn off the crate and the fawn with blood streaming down over its eye and muzzle from one of its tiny horns. The horny part had been torn off, and the base was raw. Someone had tried to steal the fawn and given up when it struggled too violently. Gabi's calm control gave way immediately to anger and anxiety, partly because he blamed himself for leaving the jeep unattended, partly because another gazelle fawn had died on him this way, after losing a horn. We dashed to Yagil's, bearing in the wounded fawn over the heads of a sampling of Beersheba's pet dogs awaiting shots. Yagil took one look at Gabi, another at the fawn, and calmly reassured us that the

injury was not serious. His bedside manner reminded me of
my doctor in Jerusalem—a soft talkative man with an
infectious optimism. Nothing, it seemed, could ever be
serious enough to look grave about; he is always smiling.

He washed the horn base, and then began cutting away the
plaster on the leg. It was a tough job, for the plaster was dry,
and, within a few minutes, the smell bad. After ten minutes of
struggling with plaster, there was no doubting why. Below
the break, the flesh was blackish purple, bleeding from a cut of
the scissors. It looked and smelled ghastly: gangrene. But
what was most disturbing was that the fawn made almost no
sound. A couple of times, a sharp otherworldly sound came
from somewhere inside it. But otherwise it lay held down,
with its head turned away from the leg. It might have seemed
completely passive except for the eyes. They were staring
wildly out of the corners of the sockets, trying to see what was
happening: the painfully wide-eyed look of an animal that
knows it is helpless to stop what is happening to it; the
resignation of pure fear.

Yagil decided to amputate the leg, and put the fawn straight
onto the operating table. The operation took thirty minutes,
with a local anesthetic in the leg, and while Yagil worked on
it, three men held the fawn down with all their strength—
careful strength, lest by weighing down too hard they break
another bone in this fragile yet incredibly strong body. For
the gazelle and many other seemingly fragile animals have a
muscle power out of all proportion to their bone structure—
three men to hold down a fawn not two feet tall.

The leg off, Yagil put a sock on the wound and stood the
fawn on its three legs. Right off the table, with half a leg
amputated under only local anesthetic, the fawn shook its
head, blinked, and stood, even moved a little. A man would
faint or be in shock.

The fawn is still in the "live collection," the miniature zoo
of the Sde Boker Field Station, and moves quite well on its
three legs. For Gabi, there was no question of whether to

amputate. He simply accepted what could be done. But as I watched the fawn on the operating table, I felt and still feel that they should have killed it. Gabi's world does not worry itself with such questions, however. What happens, happens; what can be done, is done. Beyond that, acceptance. The fawn has three legs, and for Gabi that is not a thing of sadness; it is a fact.

The day before the sandstorm, we had come into the dunes in two jeeps, at midday. One jeep had returned to base, and Gabi and I now drove off in the other to search out wood—the fragrant broom that burns glowingly and seems to imbue everything cooked on it with a smoky softness. It's the best wood for burning in the desert—a burning bush, and who knows, maybe *the* one. The smell of a broom fire has become part of the desert for me, and sweet tea cooked on it has become part of the taste of the desert.

We find two broom trees, uprooted and upended, a few hundred yards away, their branches embedded in the shifting dunes. We break off most of the branches, tug the remainder out of the sand, pile it all on the jeep, and drive back to the place where we'll sleep that night.

By now it is midafternoon. The temperature is close to 110 degrees. The sand temperature is 125, and it can go up to 160. A hot day for this part of the desert.

We go up to join the others on top of a steep dune nearby, where Udi is explaining the "sand exercise"—a twenty-four-hour spell of observation and measurement in the sand dunes, whose purpose is to correlate climatic factors with the movements of the creatures that live in the dunes. We are Udi and Gabi, a biology teacher, six high-school students, and myself. Within twenty-four hours, I will understand for the first time what relative humidity is, why desert creatures burrow, and how anything at all exists in the desert. I will work for this understanding, will even spend hours in the lab afterward charting out the correlations on graph paper, though no one told me this at the beginning or I would probably have declined the invitation to join the exercise. For the time being, all innocence, I am happy just to be here.

Udi has brought along various creatures, which he now releases so that we can watch how they move and identify their tracks. A sand tortoise, greener than the city kind and with a skirt around the rim of its shell, trundles off slowly, belly high off the sand, leaving the marks of a miniature tank. Lizards and geckos follow—a horned lizard, a flash of blue brown and gold on top and grayish white beneath, followed by the intricate gold and brown of a sand lizard. A crowned beetle dashes lightly off, leaving the fine sharp lines of its legs in the sand for us to trace. And then a sidewinder viper shimmies away from us in a continuous double-S movement, and having gained a yard or so, slowly buries itself in the sand. Sinuously, it works first its tail and then slowly the rest of its body down into the softness of the dune, moving the while in its eternal double-S, until it rests with its eyes barely peeping above the surface, the telltale trace of its curves just discernible in the sand covering it.

There is practical work to be done too: two smooth tracks of sand to be cleared, each a hundred yards by one, so that we can get a picture of which creatures live in the dunes by their tracks across the clean sand; and then the microclimate-measurement station to be set up, its array of thermometers and gauges measuring everything from the temperature a foot below ground to wind speed. This "hard work" done, we take off over the dunes. I revert happily to age ten, running and leaping in the sand until I find out that you cannot run up sand dunes. At least I can't. I can run and leap over them and down them, but not up them. So I start placing my feet very carefully, flat-footed, on the wind side, and when I'm lucky the packed sand holds my weight so that instead of sinking in at each step I gingerly glide up to the top for the sheer pleasure of leaping off down into the hollow before the next dune. Soon I have "the patent," as the Israelis say—walking carefully, slowly, flat-footed up the dunes and along the ridges, my sneakers doing sterling service. I am suddenly aware of the multiple tracks in the sand, leading into evèry scrub bush, around every thornbush, into the openings of burrows. Gabi finds a snake's tracks, and we follow them to a nest under a small dune topped by a saltbush. We post two students there to spot the snakes as they come out after nightfall. (In any event, the snakes will be far wilier than the students, who will sit there all night only to find in the morning that the snakes have burrowed themselves a fresh exit on the other side of the dune.)

The few plants here are carefully spaced, as if someone had judiciously dropped seeds each the same measured distance from the other. In these dunes, that distance is some twenty yards. Each plant thus has its own space from which to draw moisture for its roots, and no two plants overlap. The broom is one of the craftiest of these bushes, for it has multiple roots that trip you up if you're not careful: they have rerooted all around the bush as a precaution against the shifting sands. If some roots are uncovered, there will always be others to give the bush sustenance. My growing sense of purpose existing in things that have none is unsettling.

A shrike, the dramatic black-and-white bird with long bill, known also as the butcher bird for its effective work killing snails, small lizards, and rodents, perches atop one thornbush, singing loudly. As we look, it hops to another. Udi and Gabi exchange glances, and as the rest of us follow the shrike from bush to bush, they backtrack to a bush near the first one and call us over. About five feet off the ground, in the very center of the bush, is the shrike's nest. There are four chicks in it. All four act as if they are completely unaware of us: they sit stock still, not a sound from them. Fake death, their message seems to be, and we'll survive. The mother shrike must have known this message too, yet she risked herself to divert attention as far as possible away from her chicks. She needs every trick at her disposal, for standing there gazing at the chicks, I can only think of how exposed they are. True, it is a thornbush, and a thick one at that, and the nest is high off the ground. And true too, the nest is deep. But I feel uncomfortable watching the chicks and carefully close the bush behind me as I back out.

The sun is lower now, and shadows are forming among the dunes, which change from a bright pale dun to an increasingly golden yellow. I spot a lizard darting across a hollow and try one of Udi's leaps for it—getting a mouthful of sand for my pains. I emerge from the sand with the newfound knowledge that lizard catching is not for soft-handed people: the dunes are full of a short prickly kind of wild wheat, and whenever you grasp a handful of sand, you find the prickles of wheat sticking out from between your fingers where the skin is softest.

But I shall catch my first lizard after all. Just a little more organization is required for novice lizard hunters. Udi leads us along lizard tracks in the sand, moving with increasing speed from bush to bush as the tracks get clearer, until we find the place where the tracks are freshest—and where there are none leading out of the bush. We poke among the thorns (they always seem to shelter in thornbushes) to flush the lizard out. And out it comes, darting right toward me so quickly that I move without even thinking, cup my hands, dive into the sand, and close my palms against each other in a hollow. Eureka! I can feel the look of tender triumph on my face as I come up with hands still cupped, full of sand, feeling the movement of a live creature inside them. Slowly, I let the sand run out through my fingers and open my hands a little at the top, between the thumbs. I peer in, and there is an intricately patterned spotted sand lizard, perhaps some six inches long. I move thumb and fingers to grasp it above the head and alongside its belly, holding it up for all to see, inordinately proud of "my first lizard." I am yet to find out that that pride is a feeling that never quite leaves me, that every time I catch a living creature there is a tender pride in the catching, and a dangerous sense of loss and generosity in letting it go. Yes, letting it go. For the unspoken law of the field-station people is that you always let a creature go, whatever it may be, unless it is injured or in danger from humans. You may catch, look, feel, finger, but you may not interfere. So, I let the creature go, and there is no longer such a thing as "my lizard."

As the sun sets, the group gathers again to take a collective set of measurements, check the tracks (so far mainly lizards and a plethora of beetles and crowned ants), and sweep them clean once more. We set traps, arraying about twenty alongside the tracks—the "humane" kind with a trapdoor and food inside. But instead of priming them with cheese as I'm used to doing for mice, we prime them with humous, the Middle Eastern chick-pea paste, on bread. I find it hard to imagine gerbils being attracted to humous, but my imagination will be proved lacking. . . .

Gabi already has a meal going on the broom fire at camp, and we wolf down a mess of eggs, tomatoes, onions, and sausage. Then there's the age-old pleasure of relaxing around the fire with cup after cup of tea, cooked in the field-station version of the Beduin way: in a kettle often washed out inside but assiduously left with every layer of soot on the outside, filled with water, a handful of tea, and two handfuls of sugar, and placed on the fire. When the water boils up and lifts off the lid, you slip a branch under the handle and sling it off the fire—or grab it by hand, as Gabi inevitably does.

We lie around the sweet-smelling fire for a couple of hours, singing a little, talking, just lounging and staring into the fire or lying on our backs in the softness of sand. Cups of tea are passed back and forth as we swap stories and songs until the time comes for a "night round." For the first time, I see Gabi and Udi forgo sandals or bare feet for boots—a precaution against snakes and scorpions. We check the microclimate station and examine the tracks. Jerboas, the kangaroo rats that survive in the desert without drinking any water, have been out, the strong thrust of their hind legs clear in the smooth sand tracks. But since they are canny enough to live without water, they also know how to avoid traps. We find only gerbils in the traps, and in the process of extracting them and checking their sex, Udi loses his shirt to their fleas.

Soon we're tracking lizards again, by flashlight. We crawl from bush to bush across the dunes, finally racing on all fours after a thin-skinned sand lizard, which freezes the minute we catch it in the light and breathes deeply, its skin luminous with reflected color. If lizards can have heart attacks, I think, this one will, to judge from the depth and pace of its breathing. We avert the flashlight. It stays stock still another few seconds, and then disappears.

We neither see nor hear the foxes or hyenas, though there are some here in the dunes. I miss their company, but no matter which way I look I see no double red points of eyes peering toward us. There is just the dark mist of the horizon to the southwest—the only direction where there is complete darkness—and the sharper definition of the horizon in all other directions, where the lights of distant settlements create faint pools of yellowish haze, making an unnaturally sharp separation of earth and sky.

The moon will rise late tonight, so we are grateful for three pinpoints of light to guide us: the fire at camp, the tiny pool of light from the flashlight of the students camped out by the snakes' nest, and the glow of the kerosene lamp by the measurement station. We trip over thorns we'd carefully skirted earlier, fall into hollows we'd leaped into before, and finally slip and slither unseeing down the long dune to camp, and so to bed.

The Milky Way is clear and thick, the stars plentiful. A shooting star falls. I wish. And fall asleep flat out on the ground, my kaffiyeh draped over face and hands against sand flies. I fall straight into that deep, utterly refreshing sleep that only comes to me outdoors and in the absolute silence of the desert, and come wide awake about three in the morning curled into the sand, as one of the students, sleepless, builds up the fire. I rise, take a cup of tea from the black kettle, and sit with him, watching the bright half-moon fade into insignificance as the light pales the eastern half of the sky. The two of us go up to the measurement station and read off thermometers and gauges. Later, we'll realize from our charts that this is the time—just before and after dawn—when all the temperatures are closest to each other, when there is the least difference between that of the burrow and that of the surface. At this one time of day, the harsh desert climate of extremes is at its mildest. And because the desert extremes lose their power at dawn, this is the time for most creatures to emerge.

There is no wind; everything is very quiet and still. Only the tracks on the ground are evidence of how much life there is around us. But the stillness becomes disquieting as the sun rises. An eerie sunrise: no oranges, no pinks or purples, just a diffuse silvery hue over all, a white light that drains the land of color. Again and again I look up at the sky. Just above the horizon, the sun is clouded over. The clouds seem to emanate from the sun, spreading out from it into the center of the sky. As the sun rises farther it passes behind them, fringing their edges bright silver. Filtered through the cloud cover, the light becomes still more eerie.

The rising wind is hardly perceptible at first. I see it rather than feel it, for it is not a cold wind. But as the minutes pass, there seem to be fewer and fewer tracks on the ground, and it takes some more minutes to realize that this is not for lack of life, but because the tracks are being swiftly erased by the shifting sand, by grains flying lightly over the surface. The silvery light of the sun becomes paler now, and paler still, and the distant mist thickens until suddenly the horizon is no longer there, lost between glance and glance in the mist of flying sand. Now I can feel the wind picking up speed. My kaffiyeh flaps past my cheek, and my shirt catches at my side. I can see as far as the nearest range of hills; but as I look, the hilltops mist over and the mist advances toward me as if I were rapidly going shortsighted. I can hear the wind now, the high whine starting around my ears as the hot dry mist thickens. The air becomes gray, then yellow. Soon we can see the sand flying past us, feel it flying against our faces, watch as our own tracks disappear behind us. The air around us is now a mass of fast-flying grains of sand, a thick yellow mist of stinging particles that fly at us from all directions. I can feel sand stinging my back under the shirt, against my calves under the jeans, against the nape of my neck. I think of the shrike chicks: how will they fare in this storm? But I cannot find the tree to see how they are, and I fear to wander too far lest I lose sight of the others and of my direction.

There is no tracking to be done in these conditions, so we gather up all the traps we've laid, checking and rechecking their number lest we leave one by mistake and some creature caught in it either roasts or starves to death. We release the six gerbils caught in the traps, and they dash immediately for cover. We make for the camp, where Gabi has breakfast and the loyal kettle going. I rearrange my kaffiyeh pseudo-Beduin style—the side of the square straight across the forehead, the corners of that side tied behind my head at the bottom of the skull, and the rest pulled down loose over neck and shoulders, so that when I'm facing into the wind I can pull one corner up and around over my mouth and nose and tuck it in again behind at the other side.

As visibility decreases, now down to some thirty yards, Udi and Gabi decide to call off the sand exercise. Most of the students are complaining bitterly. I want to stay and wait out the storm sitting just as I am in the lee of a dune, tea in one hand and cigarette in the other, gazing into the haze of sand around me and waiting for my dreams to come waltzing out of it, over the dunes, as Fellini's do in his films. True, I love all storms, and can stand for hours watching lightning or walk for hours in a snowstorm. And I'm enjoying this sandstorm with that same delight in extremes, in the wildness of weather, but with the extra pleasure of the harmony of a sandstorm in the dunes.

And then as if in answer to my thirst for dream images, Steve, an American student with long straight black hair and a leather thong tied around it, rises and goes up to the top of a nearby dune. Standing apart thus, he unwraps a huge black-and-white prayer shawl of the Cohanim, the priestly caste of Judaism, and throws it over his shoulders. It flows past him in the wind, creating a powerfully ritualistic image as he binds his forearms and forehead with the leather thongs of his phylacteries and begins his morning prayers. It looks absolutely in place. No longer is it a mere throwback to ancient times, when the Israelites were a nomadic tribe in this very desert. The flow of time and place makes of it a dramatic and powerful mode of existence, of finding the inner strength to face the elements of the desert. As I watch, Steve becomes an archetypal figure, a desert vision entirely elemental but making perfect sense. A figure shawled in black and dwhite, standing on a rise against the wind, against the flying sand, asserting the primacy of his faith.

Meanwhile, Gabi has organized the other students to break camp. By the time he gets the equipment and as many people as possible onto the single jeep, it must be some three hours after dawn. To my delight, there is not enough room for everyone. Udi, two students, and I volunteer to walk out. Gabi will not be able to find the way back to us through the storm, so he'll meet us later with the jeep, some miles away on the nearest road.

The pitch of the wind is so strong now that even before we lose sight of the jeep, we can no longer hear it. .With only four of us left, and the jeep and equipment all gone, the storm sounds suddenly louder, the wind fiercer. But we have water, and Udi knows the terrain; and the idea of walking through the storm gets me to my feet, water bottle over shoulder, kaffiyeh over mouth and nose, eager to move through it.

We walk slowly. We have no reason to go fast. Soonwe hit a strip of packed-down sand that meanders along through the hollows of the dunes. In the days when there were still empires, this was part of the British army track that led from Beersheba to Ismailia, linking the Negev to the northern Sinai and to the coastal route through to Cairo and Alexandria. Two months ago, I drove through a sandstorm on that route, near El Arish. It was less severe than this storm. But I remember that as I watched the sand swirling over the asphalt and as I swerved to avoid sand drifts and strove for vision, I was glad that I was driving and not walking. Yet now I'm completely happy that I'm walking, and suddenly I can imagine no more absurd way of dealing with a sandstorm than driving through it. Driving, I saw sand, but saw and felt nothing of what the sand can do. Protected by the metal frame of the car, all senses other than sight had cut off the storm so that it was demeaned to the level of a driving hazard or at best to a blank yellow screen for my imagination.

Here, walking in the storm, the dunes are rich beyond imagination. The occasional sun-bleached skulls of goats and other creatures take on a new aura of impersonal possibility, the bones pitted by the flying sand. Udi picks up the dried-out body of a sand lizard. It looks like a human fetus, curled in on itself as though the last drop of moisture had been at its very center. I put it into one of the breast pockets of my shirt. I spot the front half of a sand tortoise, like the lizard almost weightless with dehydration. That goes into my other pocket. As I move, I feel the two, lizard and tortoise, flapping with the wind against my body. We walk on, eyes blanketed by sand, ears by wind, our bodies sheltering niches of their own in a lost world.

My sense of time has long gone, but I feel a deep pang of "too soon, too soon" as the track leads us out of the dunes to a dry creek near Kibbutz Revivim. And so we finally emerge onto the narrow road—Udi with his flea-infested shirt slung over his shoulder, I with two dehydrated bodies in my breast pockets, all four of us with sand thick in our eye sockets and mouths, eyes red, mouths dry. Across the road we see the form of a man moving through the swirling sand. We walk over, the outline of a peach orchard becoming clearer as we approach. A few kibbutz members are working rapidly on the

trees, anxious to get the fruit off them in this weather. We beg
a peach each, and lying on a sandbank by the road, we eat
them. I have never been so aware of how large, how ripe, how
golden, how juicy a peach can be. A puritan side of me
maintains that it is absurd to sit eating a peach in a sandstorm,
but a stronger, more innocent part of me laughs in delight,
unaware of absurdity and happy to accept the magic of such a
thing in such a place.

We plant the peach pits in the sand, much as we would
plant all manner of pits and seeds when we were children, full
of the hope that they might grow into trees—only to forget the
next day, as children do, that we'd even planted them. And
then we lie back, tired, and chat desultorily until the jeep
comes into sight and Gabi, as sand-filled and red-eyed as we,
takes us back to Sde Boker.

4 · Hermits

In the Christian Quarter of the Old City of Jerusalem, there is a tiny store painted bright blue. It has no fixed hours, but more often than not, it is open. The owner, a wizened Greek Orthodox man with a tiny high voice, welcomes me each time I go there as if we had only just met. He no longer remembers people so well but he knows exactly what is in his store, and where in its two packed rooms it may be found.

It was the postcards that first attracted me. Passing by those cluttered windows one day, I looked in out of curiosity, and seeing the assemblage of jumble inside, stayed for a few hours, sorting through some of the millions of postcards and putting to one side the old sepia-colored ones of "native girls" baring a breast to the photographer, of General Allenby's triumphant entry into Jerusalem in 1918, of ladies and gentlemen gazing into each other's eyes under a forsythia-garlanded bower, and of Jewish pioneers baring muscles in the fields or proudly riding their steeds on defense patrol.

Most of the cards were stacked against one of the walls of the inner room, from floor to ceiling. Some were in boxes; others roughly bundled together with elastic bands. To get them out onto the counter, I had to reach through the olive-wood camels and Jesuses piled together on the shelves in front of them, through the incense and the buttons, the Moslem worry beads and the rosaries, the old Greek school books, the brashly colored pictures of St. George and the dragon, the priests' robes, the rings and necklaces, icons and statuettes, beads and Mickey Mouse watches—all of which are the old man's accumulation of a lifetime, his own personal love of the world assembled here in perfect disarray.

As I was searching for more cards one day, I came across a tin icon. At first I thought it was the top of a cookie tin, but since cookie-tin lids do not depict saints, it was evident that this was a poor man's icon, to be hammered onto a piece of wood and then hung on the wall. It showed an old man with a long beard, so long that it reached to his toes. He was naked, and the beard hung down to hide what should be hidden of a saint's body. He was standing erect and proud in a cave, his body strangely feminine in its curves and smoothness. Through the entrance to the cave, you could see the setting sun and a palm tree, and beyond them, red mountains. The halo around the saint's head was gold, and it glittered as it caught the light. Around the halo was an inscription, and though it was a long time since I had learned to read old Cyrillic script, I could slowly make out his name: St. Onuphrios.

The owner of the store knew little of Onuphrios other than that he had lived as a hermit in the Sinai. To me that didn't matter. I bought the tin icon for a friend who had just passed the age of sixty and was beginning to feel what he considered the burden of age. Never, I thought, could he reach the timeless age of that immensely long beard. I had no idea then that a year later, having spent most of that year in the desert, I would return to the store and ask its aging owner to help me search out another copy of the same icon, that I too would want that innocence of long beard and shining halo to hang by my desk. We searched among the postcards and found one, and now Onuphrios watches me as I write about him and those other hermits who tried to emulate him.

From the naked hills of the Judean Desert down through the Negev to the southern tip of the Sinai, there are hermits' caves high up in the rock walls of every perennial spring of water. This desert was once a haven for hermits. Before the monastery of Mar Saba was built, clinging to the walls of the

Kidron Stream between Jerusalem and the Dead Sea, hermits lived in the dozens of caves gouged into the sides of the ravine, each cave marked with a white Byzantine cross. The three monks of St. George's Monastery in Wadi Kelt, near Jericho, now leave food once a week for only one hermit, the sole inhabitant of the honeycomb of caves above the monastery. Mountain goats and strong-willed climbers can enter the hermit caves of Ein Avdat, a couple of miles from the ancient city of Avdat in the central Negev. And Mount Sinai hides hundreds of hermits' cells within its peaks and crevasses.

But the Kidron Stream no longer flows clear; its waters froth up in white foam, and only the hardiest of desert plants survive on its banks, for it now carries much of Jerusalem's industrial sewage down into the Dead Sea. The waters of Wadi Kelt were diverted into a pipeline decades ago; no stream trickles along the wadi bed, though you can hear the water in the rusted brown pipe that carries it down to Jericho. The waters of Ein Avdat still run clear, but the ancient city nearby is in ruins, abandoned since the sixth century. And even Mount Sinai no longer hides its hermits, though there are pools of water in the wadis round about and the monastery nearby is flourishing. In this whole area, there is only one hermit left to carry on the tradition of thousands of precursors fifteen hundred years ago.

The golden age of hermitry is long past. That age was the fourth century, the time of Onuphrios, to the sixth century— the span of the Byzantine era. For hermitry was a peculiarly Byzantine phenomenon. All the monastic communities that arose where hermits once lived are Greek Orthodox. The very word hermit, indeed, came from the Greek word for desert, *eremia*, since the desert and hermitry were irrevocably intertwined in the Byzantine mind.

But why the desert? One could be a hermit anywhere, it would seem. And the hills of Galilee or the shores of its lake would surely be a far more gentle atmosphere in which to commune in solitude with God. But it was neither gentleness nor softness that the hermits were searching for. For them, God could only be found in the cruelest extremes.

If the desert is frightening to many people today, it was incomparably more so in the fourth century. Walls today give us a sense of psychological security, but then they provided physical security, a solid stone safeguard against the no-man's-land and lawlessness of the wilderness beyond. Today we have walls to ensure our privacy from each other; then, the walls helped group people together against the unknown beyond. Where the unknown beyond is now each other, it was once the desert.

When Constantine recognized Christianity at the turn of the fourth century, the battle for acceptance of the new religion was over. No longer would Christians be martyred for their beliefs—no more slings and arrows, lions and wheels, racks or red-hot rods. Being part of an accepted religious institution was no challenge to the faith of those inspired by the tales of the martyrs. Eager to prove themselves, they turned to the space that they thought would test them hardest—the desert. Having faced and conquered the devils inside the city walls and driven them out beyond the walls into the wilderness, they would go out into the wilderness to do final battle with the demons, and make even that godless land clean. The old form of martyrdom was no longer possible, but now they could impose their own. Hermitry became the new form of martyrdom.

Others had left the city for the desert before the hermits—people escaping the burdens of high taxation or social condemnation by setting up small self-sufficient communities in the wilderness. The idea was not new, but for the early Christian seekers after purity, it offered a new mode of salvation. No longer persecuted, they sought out a self-inflicted persecution by venturing alone into the desert, there to face their own inner demons in the form of visionary demons with horns, tails, and fiery mouths, whom they constantly confronted. The barrenness of the desert was to mortify their flesh, help them in their battle to renounce their physical being for a purely spiritual one. The emptiness of the desert was to bring them, as one early hermit said, to the stage where "except a man shall say in his heart, 'I alone and God are in the world,' he shall not find peace."

Mount Sinai was an ideal goal for a hermit. Placed in the center of forbidding red granite peaks, in a climate where the temperature of night and day could vary by 50 degrees, where there was no rain for a year and then suddenly snow, where access was difficult and dangerous, it was yet a holy place, one where God had shown Himself and had spoken. And if to Moses and to Elijah, then maybe also to the new seekers after purity.

Onuphrios was one of the first to reach Mount Sinai. He lived not on the holy mountain itself, but in one of the ravines down below it, in a tiny cave beside a stream. He went completely naked whatever the weather, his only condescension to modesty being a garland of leaves around his loins and a luxuriant growth of both head and facial hair. As more and more hermits came to the area, his reputation spread. Pilgrims would journey to the Sinai to see him and speak with him, but he fled from everyone, never talking to a single man for the full fifty years of his hermitry. Until his last day. On that day, a young would-be hermit, who would later become a well-known abbott, was wandering the area, trying to decide if he would have the staying power to take on the hermitic life. Suddenly he saw the wild and hairy figure of Onuphrios and, convinced that this was a demon, fled. But since Onuphrios had been honed by living in the desert for fifty years, he was in far better shape than the young man; despite his age, he caught up with the terrified novice and assured him that he was no demon but a holy hermit who now, on this day, desired to talk to another human being. The young man went with Onuphrios to his cell, and there the two talked through the day of holy matters, eating dates from the date palm outside the cell together with bread that miraculously appeared in a niche inside it. At sunset, just as the last colors had left the sky, Onuphrios lay down to die, and bade the young man bury him right there, in his cell. The young man did so. When he had finished his task, he stepped out of the cave, and it collapsed behind him, while the date palm outside it faded away into nothingness.

It was on that last day of his life that Onuphrios confided the reason for his flight from other humans in a statement that was the prototypical philosophy of the hermitic movement: "He who holds intercourse with his fellow men," he said, "will never be able to speak with the angels."

There is an innocence in Onuphrios's saying that calls forth a deep response of gentle admiration in everyone to whom I have told it. Yet there is a terrible selfishness too, and I think a terrible pride. For what kind of man is it who denies men for angels, who denies his own humanity, in fact, for the inhuman, reaching for what is by definition unreachable? Perhaps, by finally speaking to a fellow man on that last day of his life, Onuphrios acknowledged the pride and futility of his life's search, and having finally made his peace not with God, but with his own humanity, he died. Perhaps, indeed, it was through his own humanity that he finally spoke with the angels. But if so, Onuphrios was one of the exceptions.

As more and more hermits gathered around Mount Sinai, many of them living in caves on the mountain itself, they began to vie with each other in asceticism. Some of the stories of survival under impossible conditions are clearly pure legend: not all the will or faith in the world will keep a man alive if he stands plaiting palms twenty-four hours a day, without food or water, his only respite being a little sleep and a meal of lettuce leaves on Sundays. But chains and near-starvation, self-flagellation and prolonged vigils were apparently par for the course on Mount Sinai. Where one hermit renounced all cooked food, another would eat only wild herbs; where one manacled his hands, another would manacle both hands and feet; where one ate only bread and water for a week, another would do so for a year. . . . The more hermits there were, the more extreme their self-mortification became; and the more extreme the stories, the more they caught the imagination of religious folk of the time. There were apocryphal figures such as the two Indian princes, brothers, who loved the same woman. They were about to fight to the death for her when, realizing their folly in a flash of enlightenment, they repaired to Mount Sinai, where they chained themselves together in a tiny cave in such a way that when one slept, his movement in lying down would pull the other up onto his knees to pray. Neither spoke another word until they died, together, after a decade of mutual mortification—a terrifying early version of Sartre's *Huis Clos* vision, "hell is other people."

The hermit cells are still there, though a bit of rock climbing is needed to get to them. Some of them are like miniature houses built into the rock face. Others are no more than a natural hole in the rock walled off on one side against the elements. Many of them are quiet and peaceful places to be; some are so small that you can only sit in them, crouching behind the wall and peering out like an animal in its lair at the expanse of mountains and sky outside. One is somewhat more sophisticated than most: it is high up above the center of the mountain, over a narrow ridge of rock, and even when I stood in front of it I would not have seen it were it not for the small cistern nearby. It was just a tiny opening in the rock face. I squeezed in, and unable to stand, sat down at the back of the cave, where the rock formed a kind of natural throne. Behind and above me was a long niche in the rock where I could place my belongings. And that was all. The cave was so small that I could not stretch out to sleep if I wanted to, but would have to sleep as the hermit who lived there must have done, curled like a fetus into the rock. I could see nothing of the view outside, just the sky through the narrow entrance of this rock pit. And though I sat there for a while, feeling the excitement of sitting where centuries before me a holy man had sat a lifetime through, I knew I could not stay there for long. It was a cell to me—a jail cell and not a holy one. Instead of solitude, I felt claustrophobia. I wondered what would happen to my mind if I lived in a place like that. Would I really become closer to God? Or would my mind, cut off from sight and sound, invent its own panoply of demons and visions? I could only marvel at the willpower that would direct this hermit's thoughts toward God instead of sending him completely crazy. But then there is no indication of which way he did go, whether to mysticism or to madness.

I suspect madness. For there was something crazed about the way the hermits saw and used the desert. In fact it was a travesty of the symbiotic relationship between desert and faith in both Christianity and Judaism and, later, in Islam.

The desert was an essential part of the spiritual preparation and symbolism of most of the great prophets. Moses, Jesus, and Muhammad all spent forty days and forty nights in the desert wilderness, a time in which they cleansed themselves spiritually, refreshing body and soul in order to meet the trials and revelations to come. They went to the desert to find in that vast openness the simplicity and clarity of vision that they brought back to the world. They did not "find God" in that time, but they found the space and breadth of godliness, the awful and the peaceful combined in timeless silence. By accepting the vastness and free expanses of their surroundings, they reached the selflessness of spiritual preparation for revelation.

Throughout the three traditions, the desert is a place of preparation. The forty years of the Israelite Exodus from Egypt, wandering the Wilderness of Zin, was a time of cleansing before the entry into the Promised Land, a time ordained so that those who came out of Egypt as adults would not enter the new, clean place, but only those who were born in the cleanness of the desert: ". . . he made them wander in the wilderness forty years, until all the generation that had done evil in the sight of the Lord was consumed" (Numbers 32:13). Moses spent forty days and forty nights on Mount Sinai

neither eating bread nor drinking water until he was deemed
ready to receive the Tablets of the Law. The great flood of
Noah's ark lasted forty days and forty nights, the time needed
to cleanse the land and make possible a new start. Elijah
traveled forty days and forty nights through the desert from
Beersheba to Mount Sinai. Moses lived in the spiritual void of
Pharaoh's court for forty years until he discovered his origins
and fled. Jesus fasted forty days and forty nights in the Judean
Desert after his baptism, and only after that time did he face
and withstand the devil's temptations and begin his career as a
spiritual leader. Forty—whether days, nights, or years—was
always a desert period of purification and preparation. It is a
magic number, not a natural one like the lunar and menstrual
periods of thirty days, nor a holy one like seven and thirteen,
but a supernatural number that indicates preparation for
importance. It is not what happens during the "forty" that is
revelatory, but what happens immediately after it. The forty
years or days in the desert were times of preparation for return
to the world. For Moses, Jesus, and Muhammad, the desert
was not the world, but a place and time of cleansing in order
to return and meet the world with full power.

But for the hermits, the desert was the whole world and the
only world. They cared nothing for other people. "Except a
man shall say in his heart, 'I alone and God are in this world,'
he shall not find peace." This was their aim: to forget others,
not to help them. What they sought was not to create an
example by their devotion or to help purify the world by their
own actions, but the entirely personal goal of finding God
and, through God, their own redemption. Instead of the
selflessness of the desert and the tradition of their own faith,
they found only selfishness. And it was within this selfishness
that the egotistical mania of competitive mortification flour-
ished.

There were among them some few truly holy men who
found their god, like Onuphrios. But if so, I believe that it was
because they stopped searching, not because they intensified

their search. I do not believe that one can search for God, or even for oneself, in the desert. One can simply accept what is there, and through that acceptance, experience a mystic feeling of oneness and simplicity, of freedom and expansiveness that has no connection with one's own self or one's own private searchings and aspirations. The desert imposes selflessness; to the stubbornly selfish, it accords only fear, madness, or death. This was the problem of the hermits. They were searching for themselves alone, determined to find and to fight their demons, to find and to enter their god. The desert was not preparation for them. It was the final battlefield of their search for God. And I do not believe that one can find God in battle.

There is indeed godliness in the desert, but for those who accept the desert, not for those who fight it. The whole scale of time and place of the desert is utterly other, utterly apart from the time and space of the smallness of human lives. The knowledge that these rocks have been here for millions, sometimes billions of years awes and frightens many people, I know; but I find something else in them. Being aware of the agelessness and vastness of these mountains and plains seems to expand my physical presence, indeed my whole being. Instead of making me feel small and insignificant, it opens me, frees me from myself.

Only once did I "use" the desert by going into it for a selfish purpose. It was New Year's Day, the day after a very painful breakup with a long-time lover in Jerusalem. I drove south, as far into the hills of the central Negev as I could. Then I left the car, and taking just a jacket, a water bottle, two apples, and two cigarettes, I walked. I walked up and around the hills, down through the wadis, and up again until I found the highest hill in the range. I had been walking for some three hours. My plan had been to think on this walk—of our relationship, of our love and the pain it was causing us. But I found that no sooner had I left the car than there were no private thoughts in my head. I was looking and seeing, hearing and listening, sensing and feeling the hills, the wind, the sun. I was caught up in the rhythm of motion, the feel of flint stones underfoot, the patches of smooth rock on which I would lie down to rest occasionally, the vista of range after range of hills stretching away from me. On the top of the highest hill were the ruins of an ancient cairn. I sat down on top of it and carefully lit a cigarette, thinking that now I would think. And I did, for a few minutes, until the soft howling of the wind in the gorges around me entranced my attention and my eyes wandered to the purpling hills of late afternoon in the distance. I was alone. I could see no sign of people or their civilization. Just me and the desert—and an occasional buzzard. Alone, but no longer lonely. For one can only be lonely in relation to people. And being alone in the desert is to be alone *with* this expanse of wildness and wilderness, of rock and sky, stone and thorn. In loneliness, I feel closed in on myself, cut off. But in the desert, alone, it is as if I were expanding to join this vastness. Instead of being cut off, I was becoming part of it. I sat still there for some time, and as I turned to begin the walk back, I found to my surprise that I was singing softly. Instead of being immersed in my pain, I had been taken beyond it. The walk had not healed the pain, I knew, for it was a pain that would demand its own time in which to heal; but the sharp hysterical edge of it had been smoothed, leaving me with the work of mourning to be done.

I found an innocence in the desert that is larger than the loving cruelties we inflict upon each other, a timelessness and vastness that overrides the time and place of our suffering. To anyone who knows the wonder of stumbling on a wildflower suddenly blooming after a desert shower, the desert is the place of William Blake's *Auguries of Innocence:*

> To see a World in a Grain of Sand
> And a Heaven in a Wild Flower,
> Hold Infinity in the palm of your hand
> And Eternity in an hour.

If one can find this, then one can accept that "Man was made for Joy and Woe," and when the joy seems far away, accept the woe. The very knowledge that the desert transcends the personal tragedies of human beings enabled me to do this on that New Year's Day.

The feeling of that day is surely the basis of religious experience. Although I am not religious, I can see that religion is the transcendence of human emotions, of the daily inter-course of human life, for something on a larger, other plane, something beyond good and evil and beyond joy and woe. But if I see this as the basis of the religious experience, the hermits did not. Where I find a quiet transcendence in the peace of the desert, they sought utter rejection of their own humanity in what they saw as the primordial chaos—a howling dark waste inhabited by evil spirits, a realm beyond God's presence. Only within this chaos, they thought, could they prepare their souls for their own redemption—their own, and not that of other men or the world. Not for them the social conscience that brought Moses, Jesus, and Muhammad back out of their solitude to lead their fellow men. For the hermit there was only himself and his unending confrontation with the desert as the expression of all evil. Far from being beyond good and evil, the desert was his battleground against all the sins he imagined himself capable of; and as his solitude was extended, so too his imagination expanded. Little wonder, then, that for the majority of the hermits self-hate would take the place of humility, and gentleness would become masochism.

The extremes of hermitry could not last long. Those few hermits who had indeed found their peace in the desert could not remain blind to the passionate excesses being committed in the name of God by those who sought to rise above passion. It was St. Anthony, one of the first and most famous of the hermits who had spent thirty years alone in the northwestern desert of Egypt, who founded the monastic movement in the recognition that "with our neighbor is life and death." While the Egyptian desert monks combined directly into monastic communities, those of the Sinai developed an intermediate mode, the *lavra*, whereby ten or twelve hermits would submit to the authority of a charismatic figure among them known as the *abba*—the Aramaic word for "father" that would later develop into "abbott." For most of the week, the hermits lived in solitude in their cells, and then gathered together on Saturday mornings with the *abba* to pray, to exchange grains and vegetables, and to hear his rulings. There they would stay, eating and praying, until Sunday evening, when they would take whatever they needed for the coming week and return to their solitary vigils, prayers, and labors until the next weekend. By the sixth century, there were no less than three hundred hermits living on the rocky square mile of Mount Sinai, and it was entirely due to the development of the lavra system that instead of the holy mountain appearing to be a vast canvas by Hieronymus Bosch, it was a place of silent contemplation and of slow, careful physical labor, as the monks applied themselves to tending whatever crops they could and building paths and steps. They worked slowly and mechanically so that the work would not disturb their spiritual development, in the quiet knowledge that whatever they did, however long it took, it was to the glory of God, and that such work was the work of a lifetime.

By the time the monastery of Santa Katerina was founded later in the sixth century, gathering the lavras into its fold, the age of hermitry was on the decline. The yoke of the abbott's will and the friction of living among men in a communal life took the place of solitary communion. The monastery became the power, and any monks who still wished to lead the hermitic life could do so only with the abbott's permission and under his direction. The monastery institutionalized hermitry. There is the story of a respected solitary who came out of the desert to spend the rest of his days in a monastery. When asked why, he told of how, in the first days of the hermit movement, "the sparseness of those who at that time dwelt in the desert was gracious to us as a caress; it lavished liberty

upon us, in the far-flowing vastness of that solitude." But the
arrival of others eager to emulate the first restricted that
liberty, confining it to the pettiness of ascetic competitiveness.
"Sublimity was gone," commented Helen Waddell in her
account of the *Vitae Patrum*, "let him make up for it in
obedience."

What the few first holy men had found in the desert, the
many who came to emulate them had destroyed. For truly
holy men were as rare then as they are now. And the desert
does not tolerate people easily. When too many seek it, and
seek it out of hate and self-hate, when it becomes a thorough-
fare for those who imagine it cruel and demonic, it changes
from a place of quiet and vast solitude into that other, human,
desert. Most of the hermits brought their desert with them,
and they demeaned the real desert by doing so. Instead of
finding the ultimate vision that they sought, they sank further
into their own blindness. "The truth is that solitude is the
creative condition of genius, religious or secular, and the
ultimate sterilizing of it," wrote Helen Waddell. "No human
soul can for long ignore 'the giant agony of the world' and live,
except indeed the mollusk life, a barnacle upon eternity."

5 · Snails

If you wander through the hills of the central Negev in midsummer, you might think that some of the bushes have sprouted hundreds of tiny white flowers, or that white drops of manna have fallen to the ground. But look a little closer and you'll see that the white spots are a miracle of another order. They are snails—millions of white snails living in the desert, where there is as little as two inches of rainfall a year. Their only food is the algae in the crust of the desert soil, which exist only after rain. Yet they are everywhere, clinging to the sparse bushes and littering the ground.

Snails in the desert. What a perfect occasion for whimsy! Yet whimsy is utterly inadequate to water creatures living in apparent defiance of the very laws of life itself.

Life sometimes exists by the most absurd rules. The most successful desert creatures—the ones that have lived longest in the desert and whose numbers are largest—are the smallest. And among the most astonishing of these creatures are the white desert snail, a mollusk, and the desert wood louse, a crustacean. Their world is generally limited to a maximum of a few square yards, and they spend most of their life underground. A poor kind of life, it may seem, but eminently suited to the desert. For the desert is one of the most stressful environments imaginable for life, let alone water life. The two primary variables by which the desert is defined are rainfall and radiation. Rainfall is low and highly undependable. You never know if it is going to rain at all, let alone when or where. But radiation is high and extremely dependable. You know without a doubt that out in the open you are bombarded by the highest degree of thermodynamic energy on the face of the earth. And as if each of these two variables is not sufficiently forbidding in itself, they combine with sometimes terrifying force. Low rainfall and high radiation reinforce each other to create an extreme stress system for even the hardiest form of life. For the basis of all life is water. And in the absence of water, no life is possible.

Life in the desert is thus life on the brink of death. It is the outer limits of life. That, at least, is how we humans might see it, for we tend to equate the nonexistence of life with death. Unable to detach ourselves from our own concept of life and its importance, we tend to seek reassurance of our own vitality as it is mirrored in other life forms. But sometimes that reassurance is extremely tenuous. Can anthropomorphism really stretch to snails?

The snail and the wood louse are among the desert's most ancient inhabitants—and therein lies the secret of their being there at all. They are, in a sense, those that got left behind when the last Ice Age came to an end some ten thousand years ago and the waters began to recede from the deserts of the Middle East, leaving swamps and marshes that gradually dried up over the next few thousand years to form the arid deserts of today, where rain is a rare and precious phenomenon and the sun's rays beat down mercilessly on all forms of life.

Maybe they were the outcasts of their species—the most retarded or the most advanced forms. We cannot possibly know. But we do know that in order to survive in increasingly arid circumstances, these water creatures developed extraordinarily complicated mechanisms of adaptation, mechanisms "designed" to deal with high radiation and unpredictable rainfall. They survived, and they continue to do so. And the very fact of reproduction, of maintaining a stable population of water creatures in the desert, would seem to be an achievement of tremendous power and force.

Yet I don't know whether to be awestruck at their ability to survive, at the indomitable force of life against all odds, or to be dismayed by the contortions and the apparent pointlessness of life for life's sake. I see through human eyes, and my values are human values. Inevitably, anthropomorphism colors my thinking. Survival is not enough for me, neither survival of the species nor survival of the ecosystem of which it is a part. It is a biological phenomenon that achieves meaning only if I can see things in terms of "survival in order to . . ." In order to enjoy it, in order to create, in order to struggle. . . . There are as many reasons for survival as there are humans. I search for meaning in survival, and not finding any in human terms, I refuse to accept it for what it is and call it absurd. But then the very terms of my humanity make the absurd admirable. For as humans we are the only creatures that are *aware*, as far as we know, of life and death—of the fragility and tenacity of life and of the possibility of death. And this surely is part of the awe and admiration we feel when we look at such creatures as the desert snail and the wood louse. For we are looking at survival under conditions where we, humans able to grasp the conditions of existence of another species, would have simply given up.

Some friends in Jerusalem once had a pet snail. They kept it in an ashtray filled with water-soaked cotton wool and fed it an array of greenery from their garden, until the day it crawled out of the ashtray and over an open copy of the collected works of Sigmund Freud, eating through the top five pages as it went. . . .

But snails in the desert have no such water-soaked habitat, nor abundant greenery to live on, let alone the written word of Freud. In fact, no one knows exactly how they survive. Two scientists at the Desert Research Institute in Sde Boker, Moshe Shachak and Yossi Steinberger, have been studying them for twelve years altogether, and in great detail for the last seven. For every question they ask, they say, five more turn up. Yet the incomplete picture that emerges from the most basic questions is sufficiently amazing.

The most salient fact about snails, for me at least, is that they are hermaphrodites. For a while, I was indulging in wonderfully anthropomorphic fantasies about the sex life of snails until I realized that the only reason that snails are hermaphroditic is that every snail can then lay eggs. The reproductive capacity of the species is simply doubled. So much, I thought, for sex in the desert.

The next most salient fact about these snails is that they are active only 5 percent of each year. They move, mate, eat, and drink for an average of only twenty days a year, sometimes as little as eight days, sometimes as many as twenty-seven, depending on that year's rainfall. They spend the rest of the time in estivation (the summer equivalent of hibernation), existing at the lowest possible metabolic level.

Their life cycle starts during estivation, when there is only one organ in their bodies that does not sleep. That organ is the sex gland. Throughout estivation, it produces sperm. With the first rain—which may be the only rain—the snails come out of estivation. But after a year without food or water they neither eat nor drink. They mate, immediately. When they start mating, their sex glands switch from male to female, and start producing eggs. Since the sex organ of each snail is both male and female, mating is a process of mutual impregnation. Only after impregnation is achieved do the snails separate and start seeing to their own individual survival, feeding on the algae that grow in the desert topsoil after rain, and drinking.

As one might expect, the snail eats and drinks with a vengeance. It can eat enough within a day and a half to last it a year, since the minimal metabolic level of estivation means that a store of food that would last a relatively short time for an active life will last far longer for a nonactive one. And being a desert creature, it eats more than a year's supply if it can, for the next year's rainfall is by no means guaranteed. Its drinking capacity is even greater. It can absorb 406 microliters of water a day when it needs only 0.5 a day on estivation—a very wide margin, which allows for its high water loss during the days when it is active.

When the soil dries out again in the winter sun, the snails retreat once more into estivation, spinning a thin membrane over the entrance to their shells. They stay on the surface, relying on their white shells to reflect most of the radiation. And so they remain until the next rain—if there is a next rain. Then they lay their eggs. But the extraordinary thing is that the snails can "choose" when to lay their eggs. If the second rain comes within thirty days of the first, they do not lay any eggs; they simply wait until the third rain, if that is at least thirty days after the second. And if there is no thirty-day gap between rains, or if it is a drought year and no more rain falls at all, then the snails simply reabsorb the unlaid eggs into their bodies and stay in estivation, apparently waiting for better luck the next year.

If there is a second rainfall at least a month after the first, each snail lays thirty to forty eggs in a small sac an inch or two below the soil surface. They choose the areas that stay wet longest in which to lay the eggs. But the researchers cannot figure out how the snails know which areas these are. A flat loess surface, for instance, looks as though it would retain water at an even rate throughout, yet some parts of it dry out before others. While the researchers cannot predict which areas these will be, the snails apparently can, for only there do they lay their eggs.

One could now argue that all this adds up to an excellent strategy for increasing the probability of reproduction under highly improbable conditions. With such an extraordinary sensitivity to humidity, it seems that the snails would be able to multiply at an incredibly rapid rate even in the desert. But the desert has yet to have its say. Laying eggs is one thing; the incubation of eggs into snails and then the survival of snails to lay more eggs, is quite another.

Within a month of laying, half the eggs hatch. These are the survivors of the underground battle for humidity. The others simply dehydrate and shrivel into empty husks. The young snails, barely a fifth of an inch in diameter, remain underground throughout the summer, though how they manage to extract sufficient humidity from the soil during the long heat is still unknown. They emerge into daylight for the first time only with the first rain of the following winter.

Daylight has its own dangers, however. Once on the surface the young snails have a minimal chance of survival; their shells are still soft. They are easy prey for rodents, lizards, and birds—especially the song thrush, which pauses on its migratory route to prey on both young and adult snails. It takes a snail in its beak and, elegantly tossing its head upward, suddenly thrusts down against a stone, breaks the snail's shell, and reaches the watery morsel inside.

Snails thus have a very high attrition rate. It might be possible to work out the balance of survival if it was known how long they live. But no one knows this. The research scientists quickly found out that the old saw about telling a snail's age from the rings in its shell was useless. All they can say is that snails live at least twelve years, because they first started marking snails twelve years ago, and some of those snails are still alive. The most that can be said is that given the tough climatic conditions together with the predator rate, there is a fair chance of one snail out of each batch of thirty to forty eggs surviving over twelve years, the maximum known life-span of a snail. In other words, the snails just manage to reproduce themselves.

What a poor conclusion for such a contorted life cycle! Over twelve years, a snail leads an active life for a mere 240 days and only just manages to enable one more snail to do the same. It begs the question of whether desert survival would not be a far simpler matter if there were a lower birth rate combined with better organization for survival of individuals. The desert wood lice answer this question. These tiny inch-long gray crustaceans have a definite form of birth control combined with a well-defined family life. Yet their story is every bit as strange as that of the snails.

Desert wood lice are more correctly known as isopods. At least, that is the term the scientists use, perhaps because there are no woods in the desert. Yet to me they are more alive as wood lice than as isopods. It would have felt odd to sit in the cold white light before sunrise waiting for something so correct as an isopod to emerge from its burrow. Knowing that these creatures were wood lice gave those times of shivering waiting some of the absurd curiosity of life, soon to be satisfied as dozens of them would stream out of each burrow and beetle off, each in its own straight line, toward the nearest piece of dried plant matter. Like the snails, it makes not a whit of difference to the wood lice if they are observed or not. They are not programmed to worry about the existence of other potentially dangerous species. Automatically, they continue with their job, which is to clean the desert.

Wood lice are neither hermaphrodites nor estivators. The most important fact about wood lice is that they excrete. They eat organic material—dry plant matter and dry algae and bacteria in the loess soil itself. This way, their alimentary systems are the means of transferring dried plant matter back into the soil. When their excreta mingles with the soil, microorganisms can start the work of decomposition, thus "enriching" the soil—a very relative term in the desert—and enabling more plant matter to grow. The wood lice thus play a vital role in the desert ecosystem, acting as a kind of public-transport service in the process of mineral cycling. In this service, the wood lice eat and excrete the whole of the desert topsoil at least once every one hundred thousand years. In other words, desert soil is the multiple excreta of wood lice.

Besides being one of the most ancient desert species, the wood louse is also one of the few species found throughout the deserts of the Old World (Asia and Africa). Its solution to the problem of survival is radically different from that of the snail. Instead of reproducing to the limit in the hope that some of its offspring will survive, it limits its reproductive activities. It practices a form of birth control.

Its life cycle starts at the beginning of February. At that time, no matter what the climatic conditions, no matter whether it has been a drought year or one with relatively high rainfall, the wood lice emerge from their burrows, spreading out in different directions, and start eating. Only after eating do the females among them start digging shallow burrows where they wait for males to come "courting" them. But the curious thing is that not all the females dig a burrow; and if a female does not dig a burrow, no male will come courting her. Depending on the climatic conditions, only 5 to 20 percent of the females dig burrows—and no one knows how this selection is decided and carried out. The males then come visiting those females available for mating. If two come courting the same female, they may fight; the winner, most sensibly, is the one who manages to flip the other over onto its back!

But the price paid by the losing wood louse is more than the mere ignominy of lying on its back waving its legs in the air until it rights itself again. Nonmating wood lice, both male and female, die immediately. If they have no reproductive role, then the wood-louse life cycle allows them no role at all. Only those that reproduce are allowed to complete the full thirteen to fifteen months of their life cycle.

The surviving wood lice are monogamous couples. Once paired, they exchange a certain chemical so that they can identify each other by smell. They then create a very strong family structure by transferring this smell to their young once they are hatched. The burrow is strictly a family burrow. No stranger is allowed in or, indeed, would want to enter. The purpose of the smell is to enable the wood lice to identify their own burrow—no easy matter when there may be as many as two or three per square yard. It allows them to find their way home.

Each female lays about eighty eggs, which hatch at the

beginning of March. The young wood lice start working immediately. Like their parents, they sortie from the burrow for a couple of hours every day, at a time that becomes earlier and earlier as the radiation increases toward late summer, when they sortie at first light. Now it is that their extraordinary digestive system serves not only the desert's survival, but also their own. For by eating, drinking, and burrowing all in the same action, they escape the extreme radiation of the summer sun and save themselves from dehydration. As the summer progresses, the wood-louse family gradually deepens its burrow, from one to two inches in February to some twenty inches by the end of the summer. When inside the burrow, they eat the loess soil, digest the algae and bacteria in it and extract any moisture from it, and then excrete it in the form of tiny dry almost-cubical pellets, which they push up onto the surface. By eating, they burrow deeper into the earth, and by burrowing, they survive. The surface ground temperature in summer may reach 150 degrees or even higher. In the depths of the burrow, the maximum temperature is 85. But one wood louse eating alone could not possibly burrow down that deep. Family life thus provides an ample supply of "working mouths."

By autumn, the young wood lice are grown to full length and their parents have died, their bodies eaten by their young. As winter comes in, they close up their burrow and stay inside it, for once the temperature inside goes down below 50, they need no food to survive. They hibernate until the beginning of February—always that time, never later and never earlier—and then they begin the cycle again, each year another generation. Like the snails, they too have just managed to reproduce themselves.

Both the snail and the wood louse survive in the desert by an extraordinary combination of flexibility and inflexibility. Behavioral adaptation has apparently led to the development of time clocks and climatic sensors that make these creatures far more sophisticated than their relatives, the nondesert species of snail and wood louse. It is their flexibility—their adoption of what the scientists call "life-history strategies"— that allows them to live in the desert. But there is the rub—in that word *allows*. For to me it seems that they are there on sufferance, living on the very fringe of existence because, perhaps, *something* has to be there to define that fringe. Yet I fear the bolt from the blue for hubris here. The snails and the wood lice have survived in the desert far longer than any human civilization. How then can I, a human, impose my human concept of life on them and judge? For they are desert creatures. And humans are not.

Existentialism might be a better approach than anthropomorphism. Albert Camus argued in *The Myth of Sisyphus* for recognizing and accepting the absurdity of life. "It is not a matter of explaining and solving," he wrote, "but of experiencing and describing. Everything begins with a lucid indifference. . . . Science, having reached the end of its paradoxes, ceases to propound and stops to contemplate and sketch the ever virgin landscape of phenomena. The heart learns thus that the emotion delighting us when we see the world's aspects comes to us not from its depth but from their diversity. Explanation is useless, but the sensation remains and, with it, the constant attractions of a universe inexhaustible in quantity."

6 · Camels

The emblem of the Israeli army's Camel Corps bears a winged camel. Against a black background, the sand-colored creature leaps skyward on white wings almost as large as its body—a desert Pegasus. Below it is a tiny jeep, earthbound—added, it seems, as an afterthought.

Under this proud emblem I learned the pleasures and perils of riding a camel. The flowing white robes and gleaming sabers of the traditional camel rider were missing, and khaki and Uzzi submachine guns seemed poor substitutes indeed. But once we were mounted—a Beduin tracker, two regular army officers, and myself—there was a definite air of professionalism about our small camel train as we wended our way out of the base camp into the sand.

We were in the dunes south of the Bardawil Lagoon, the huge seawater lake nearly closed off from the sea by a finger of land flicking up and around the shoreline between El Arish and Ismailia in the northern Sinai. East, west, and south of Bardawil stretch the classic sand dunes of desert reveries, rising and falling into the distance in regular rhythm as though the earth had left behind the pattern of its deep breathing.

This was a routine border patrol, for straight through these dunes ran a demarcation line. Sometimes a fence, sometimes just empty white oil barrels placed a hundred yards from each other, the line separated Israeli-held territory from the buffer zone inhabited, for the time being, by United Nations forces. On the other side of the buffer zone was Egypt. We were patrolling for infiltrators and smugglers, and thus the guns and khaki.

Attiyeh, the pint-sized tracker in charge of the camels that day, had greeted me warmly and courteously, making no comment on the thought of a woman on one of his camels. Quite the contrary, his deep brown eyes sparkled generously; he twirled his luxuriant black handlebar moustache with happy pride and busied himself with many a "*Krrr*" and "*Grrr*" to rouse the camels and saddle them. He assigned me a tall white camel; that is, it was more or less white if seen from a distance, and certainly white when compared to the sand-colored camels more common in the area. It was a fine camel, he assured me, an Egyptian raider that had fallen into Israeli hands in the 1973 Yom Kippur War. What he did not tell me at that point was that out of deference to my sex he had picked out the quietest and most gentle camel in the army's flock for me, and that the reason this once-fierce raider was so gentle was because at eighteen years old he was somewhat past his prime.

All the army camels are males, since female ones are far too valuable to use in this part of the world for something so minor as army patrols. Thoroughbred racing camels are always female; they are the swiftest racers, the most fearless raiders, and the most dramatic performers in the annual fiestas of camel racing held among the Beduin. And even a mongrel female is highly prized. Beduin can live off the milk alone if need be, indeed can even dry it and preserve it for months. But far more important, a female camel assures an annual 100 percent profit on the original investment, since each year she gives birth. The army does not mind that it is deprived of the best racers. It needs the camels not for their speed, but for the silence with which they move, assuring the element of surprise, and their mobility, which can take the rider to places beyond the reach of the most sophisticated jeep.

We rode northeast through the huge dunes, mountains of sand on either side. Here and there were groups of date palms, salt flats with patches of water shimmering in the early-afternoon sun, the round reed huts of the local Beduin, and then finally, as we approached the sea, that long, bony finger of land curled in the distance around the Bardawil Lagoon. Under Attiyeh's patient tutelage, I learned to ride a camel.

It was surprisingly comfortable. One can sit as one would on a horse, with legs hanging down either side of the animal's belly, or one can sit with one leg crossed over the front pommel of the saddle and hooked under the other leg alongside the camel's neck—a far more comfortable perch, which brings you higher up on the camel and gives you greater control. You can sit upright and move back and forth with the camel's pace, or lean forward with an arm on the pommel for the suitably casual posture of the accomplished rider. But beware the back pommel. Well padded, it might well be a restful support, but it is bare wood, so that when I moved back in the saddle I was careful to shift my weight a bit to one side, sitting slightly obliquely on my mount so that the pommel rested not on my spine but alongside it. That way it supported me comfortably; if I sat straight, it pounded mercilessly into my backbone.

The pleasure of camel riding must be close, I think, to that of gliding. The silence except for the wind in my ears, the height, the vista of dune after dune unrolling below me—all induced in me the most peaceful and utterly relaxing feeling, a dreamy suppleness aided by my back moving sinuously in tune with the camel's step in a self-induced massage. The camel's pace becomes that of the world round about, of the slow regular breathing of the dunes, of the sea in the distance, of the daily rhythm of life of the desert Beduin—a patient, gentle relentlessness that pulls me serenely into itself until my whole being becomes part of that rhythm. Moving my body hypnotically as I write, I think of how Nikos Kazantzakis described it in *Journeyings:* "The blood regulates itself rhythmically with this motion, and as the blood flows, so flows the soul of man. Time frees itself from the mathematical cubicles into which it has been squeezed by the rational Western mentality. Here . . . time rediscovers its primordial rhythm, it becomes a flowing and indivisible essence, a light mystical vertigo that transubstantiates thought into reverie and music."

Attiyeh meanwhile was in his element. While I was gliding, he was swooping. Perched on a fine feisty brown animal, his size became irrelevant, and he gloried in the height that the camel gave him as he galloped up and down in front of the rest of us, showing off with quick about-turns and sudden stops and starts. Evidently he was satisfied with my progress, which had been fairly rapid, since I had discovered that riding a camel is far easier for a woman to learn than for a man, for very simple reasons of human physiology against the hard wooden surface of the camel saddle. The camel, it seems to me, must by the nature of the saddle prefer women to men. Yet in Beduin society, women do not ride camels. Except in the oddest circumstances, that is the prerogative of men. Only once have I ever seen a woman on a camel in this part of the world, and that was during a census held by the Israeli authorities, when some Beduin brought in their parents to be counted. Since the couple were aged beyond walking, their children had placed them in huge saddlebags hung on either side of the creature's belly, the woman to the left, the man to the right, so that just the tops of their withered heads showed above the woven wool of the bags.

Now Attiyeh began to teach me how to gallop. The main principle is to stay in the saddle, since if you don't, no matter how many blankets are thrown over the wooden base, you will sooner or later smash your backside into a mess of black and blue. So Attiyeh taught me how to use my thighs around the front pommel, pressuring there for a hold, and soon I found I could gallop comfortably. It was exhilarating. Though we were far from the speed of a horse, the height and size of my mount gave me a feeling of power such as I have never experienced on horseback. The rhythm had not changed, only the pace, but that change in pace made the rhythm feel utterly different. I could hear the thud of those huge round padded feet on the sand more by feel than by sound, feel the power of them as they pounded the sand beneath us, see the ground responding to our rhythm as it sped by. Now it was the force of sandstorms that I felt, the piercing stinging of this place at its fiercest, no longer serenity but wildness, no longer silence but the throbbing soul-filling heartbeat beneath the calm rise and fall of the dunes.

But alas, my steed was no racer, and it tired long before I had had my fill of speed. I was disgusted: I wanted to fly, and my Pegasus wanted to plod. So I guided him up to the top of a steep dune, thinking to aid his weary limbs by the impetus of gravity. And sure enough, once we reached the top of that dune his head came up and I felt him quiver, as if he were remembering those former days of virile glory when he would charge down the dunes into the enemy camp. Plunging down we went, galloping at a marvelous speed, with me perched securely on his back, one hand out to the right with the headrope, the other out to my left with my camel stick beating against his withers as I delightedly yelled what I took to be blood-curdling cries to urge my mount onward—when he tripped, began falling, and sent me flying off to the right, doing an automatic double roll in the sand as I landed to avoid that huge body tumbling after me, until we came to rest sprawled side by side halfway down the side of the dune. He was up before me and lumbering off, evidently despairing of ever regaining the physical prowess of his youth. I ran after him as Attiyeh came galloping up to us, his face creased with worry as the camel began to gain on me. But by the time Attiyeh had leaped to the ground and reached us, I had caught the headrope, and the camel and I stood, breathless, facing each other in motionless mutual suspicion.

Then I noticed the blood on my right hand. Nothing hurt until I opened up the hand to look at it, and then the pain was just the sting of air on the open wound. There was a deep gash between the thumb and forefinger, bleeding profusely. In numb curiosity, I opened the hand farther, and stood staring fascinated at the white tendon gleaming in the sun, with

grains of sand rapidly turning deep red all around it. I had
obviously not let go of the headrope in time. Attiyeh, relaxed
now that his camel had been secured, looked and clucked. I
tried sucking the sand out as the others came riding up and
produced a field bandage. I clasped the thick pad of the
bandage in my fist, and they tied the khaki strips around the
back of my hand and my wrist. The wound throbbed but
didn't hurt, so we remounted and continued on our way; we
were three hours out of the base camp and there seemed little
point in turning back. But my camel had had his say. I did no
more galloping that day and adjusted to his sedate walking
pace so that by evening, when we reached camp, I was riding
in a state of weary, sandy, and happy serenity. The wind had
settled down and disappeared as the sun set and the evening
star appeared in the west, and the half-moon began to throw
our shadows onto the sand beneath us. We rode slowly,
nighttime riding, along the border—a time of peaceful silence,
with no one talking, until we saw the glimmer of the camp
lights in a hollow of the dunes and slowly and majestically
rode in to a meal of sweet tea and dates. Only later would I
suffer for my camel's fickle charge when the doctor in the
corps headquarters twenty miles to the east put five stitches
into my hand. And if ever I had doubted my identity as a
writer, that doubt was dissolved for good as he injected
anesthetic into the wound, for all I could say through the pain,
aside from curses, was "Will I be able to write?"

But that afternoon, remounted and riding again, no such
thoughts entered my mind. I rode with the injured hand
thrown across the front pommel, and soon forgot it in that
entrancing rhythm of camel and sand, sun and clear air. We
cut north and over to Rumiya, a dune lookout high over the
lagoon. The handful of soldiers stationed there were bored,
and our arrival was an event. They spent most of their time
watching the Egyptian fishermen in the lagoon through a
high-powered telescope, making sure that none would come
ashore. But sometimes life was a little more lively, as when

they spotted inner tubes floating ashore and picked them up on the beach to find them stuffed with hashish. This continued for some weeks, tube after tube of hashish floating straight into the hands of the Israel Defense Forces, for it apparently took some time for the message to get through that it was not the Beduin but the army who was picking them up. The hash was coming from Lebanon, not Egypt; since the Lebanese conflict had made it hard to unload shipments off the northern shores of Israel or over the well-defended northern border, the boats had taken the long trip south to this desert coast only to find that the desert too was defended.

Once, the main task of the Camel Corps was patrolling against armed infiltrators from Egypt. But times had changed in the Sinai and the Negev, and most of the corps's work now consisted of catching smugglers bringing hashish, tape recorders, and bales of silk into Israeli-held territory, and tea the other way, for tea is very expensive in Egypt. The army trackers and officers felt rather out of sorts about their role as customs men and consoled themselves with the thought that their main task was still patrolling the border.

The change in duty brought about a change in the basic methods of the corps as well. Though all the regular members of the corps wear the flying camel emblem as part of their uniform, few have ever even ridden a camel. The camel's wings have been clipped, and most of the patrolling is now done by jeep: the American M-151. It is a beautiful piece of machinery, with a low, wide-slung body, machine guns mounted fore and a mound of communications equipment aft, and wide tires. Let two-thirds of the regular amount of air out of the tires and you have a high-powered dune buggy that can race across the dunes at over sixty miles an hour. The jeep patrols tax their machines to the maximum, but nowhere more so than on the last dune before the base camp, which is so high and steep that you have to lean over the top to see the bottom of it. It is a point of honor that every jeep dive straight down this dune on the last lap home. No easing down obliquely, no roundabout way: straight down. It's a very dangerous maneuver and demands a superb touch on the wheel and a cool head, for the jeep must be kept dead straight. Even the slightest swerve will send it spinning around and tumbling down the dune. This jeep dive is terrifying and exhilarating, but nothing like the far more simple pleasure of pacing down the dune by foot, half running and half flying as each foot lands and takes you sliding down a few yards, head back and arms flung out on either side.

The corps now maintains as many jeeps as camels, since the jeeps are quicker and can cover a far larger area than the camels. And although I appreciate the thrills and spills of jeep patrolling, my sympathies remain entirely with the camel. Of course I am not a military person and therefore discount the efficiency of the jeep in speed and distance. But my judgment may also be swayed by the fact that my main mode of transport in the desert was neither the camel nor the jeep, but a Citroen Deux Chevaux, the tiny French "two-horse" car that was once the main car in use in the Israeli army. It has two cylinders, a six-hundred-cc. engine, front-wheel drive, air cooling, and independent suspension—all of which give it an amazing ability to stay on whatever road or track you want. Short of a jeep (and it costs one-quarter the price of a jeep to run), it is the best car for the desert, since it can get deep onto sand and dirt tracks on which other cars would break an axle. But even the Deux Chevaux has its limits, and when I reached them, I would abandon it for a jeep, my own two feet . . . or a camel.

Being the owner of a Deux Chevaux is no easy fate in life. One is constantly being ribbed over the strange humped shape of the car by those who have no respect for the fact that this design has been in production longer than any other in the automobile industry. It has real headlamps—not lights set into the body of the car but separate round headlamps that sit proudly atop the hood—which seem impossibly old-fashioned to most people. It is not a car for the modernist, that is true.

But then the desert is no place for the modernist either.

In France, the Deux Chevaux is no mere motorcar; it is a cultural institution, a value system in its own right. Elsewhere, however, it receives such epithets as "a tin can on wheels" from those who get into it laughing, only to sortie some hours later with a look of respect on their faces. For the Deux Chevaux is to other cars what the camel is to the horse: the horse is swifter and more aesthetic, but in the desert it is an expensive status symbol and a practical liability. I thus have a great feeling of empathy for the camel, which is equally maligned by those who prefer aesthetic ease to practical adventure. The camel has been called "a horse designed by a committee"—an even greater libel than the "tin can" epithet, for the beauty of both car and camel is not in their appearance, but in their performance. But where the car is a cultural symbol for Frenchmen, the camel is the very basis of the vast desert culture of the Beduin.

The specifications of the camel for desert life and transport are superb. It can go anywhere in the desert, far into reaches and wastes totally inaccessible to wheeled transport. It lives off the available scrub and water in the desert, no matter how sparse that may be. The longest documented trek of a camel between watering points is nearly six hundred miles in twenty-one days, through the Empty Quarter of the Sahara, but for all we know it may be able to go farther than that. The camel, in short, is the desert creature par excellence; if one wanted to design a riding and pack animal for the desert, I doubt if one could come up with anything other than the camel.

For thousands of years, people have fantasized about the camel's ability to ride through the desert without water. Pliny thought he had it two thousand years ago when he wrote in his *Historia Naturalis* that the camel had "water sacs" in its belly, a kind of private reservoir. Since his time, practically every child in the West has heard stories of desperate travelers, their eyes glazed by thirst and desert mirages, slitting open the bellies of their faithful mounts to drink from the store therein. But the fact is that the desperate desert traveler would be in dire straits indeed if he resorted to this stratagem. Not only would he kill his camel, but he'd find little water in it and thus completely ruin his chances for survival. There is a foul-smelling greenish liquid that drains slowly out of the stomach contents of a dead camel—the same liquid that will drain out of any creature's stomach once it is killed—but certainly nothing of the order of a freshwater store such as commonly envisioned.

Though it has no water sacs in either its stomach or its hump, the camel can survive without water for up to three weeks and still cover several hundred miles of difficult terrain. Logic says that it must be storing water somehow. It definitely needs water, as is evident to anyone who has seen the impressive sight of a camel watering. On a long trek it may have lost a third of its total body weight in water. (Humans die if they lose 15 percent of their body weight in water, where the camel keeps on trekking at over 30 percent.) But within ten minutes of approaching a well or a waterhole, the camel completely replaces that loss, drinking over four hundred pints of water. Since the average adult camel weighs over one thousand pounds, this would be equivalent to an adult human drinking thirty pints of water in ten minutes. But no such equivalence exists. Humans, no matter how thirsty or dehydrated, can barely drink four pints of water within such a time limit, and they will not be able to drink more even after that, no matter if they have lost five pints or even fifteen by sweating. This inability in humans to replace the water they have lost is called "voluntary dehydration," but it is not quite as crazy as it may seem. It takes the human body days to restore serious water loss, if at all, since if a human drinks too much water too soon, the blood is thinned out and the red blood cells may burst. But the water system of the camel needs no such automatic cutoff point. Its oval-shaped red blood cells can expand to 240 times their original volume when the creature drinks, changing shape from oval to round. The red corpuscles make up the real "water-storing organ," and in their extraordinary flexibility lies the secret of the camel's stamina. By absorbing large amounts of water, they allow the camel to drink to the full extent of its water loss in just a few minutes. Equally important, they can withstand the increase in salinity as the camel loses water on a desert trek. In humans and most other mammals, the blood cells can stand a maximum of 1.1 percent salinity. Over that level, they begin to shrivel like raisins and the whole circulation system breaks down. The camel's red blood cells, however, only begin to distort when the blood is 20 percent saline—a salt concentration six times as high as that of seawater—and the camel can still function when the saline concentration of its blood is pushed as high as 50 percent!

But the camel's survival lies not only in its ability to replace lost water and to function with little water in its body; it also lies in economy of use. The most important means by which the camel economizes on water is by varying its body temperature. Where the normal range of body temperature in humans is 3.5 degrees Fahrenheit, in the camel it is 12.5. Its temperature may be as low as 94 at dawn and as high as 106 by midafternoon, the degree of fluctuation depending on the heat of the season and on the amount of water available. This means that the camel can "warm up" to a considerable extent during the day without having to use water to cool itself by sweating or panting, since the tolerable temperature limit of the environment is made relatively higher. Moreover, as its body temperature rises toward midafternoon, the hottest time of the day, the heat flow from the environment is less than in other creatures, since the difference between the environmental temperature and the body temperature is smaller. Where in humans such a rise in body temperature would be the sign of a total breakdown in heat dissipation—the "heat stroke" or "explosive heat rise" that leads to death—in the camel it is part of the water-conservation mechanism.

One of the basic principles of desert life, however, is never to rely on only one mechanism. Accordingly, the camel's whole body is built to conserve an economic water regime. Both the cow and the camel, for instance, can absorb four hundred pints of water at one drinking. But where the cow uses up all this water within a day and a half, the camel can make it last two or three weeks. By a subtle interplay of hormones controlling water and salt release, it regulates the use of the water in its own body. Even the camel's fur, that matted layer that is thickest over the hump and thinnest on the belly, acts as a sophisticated form of insulation. The camel sweats only under conditions where humans would already be dead or in the throes of heat stroke; then it starts sweating lightly, just enough to cool the skin surface under the fur. The matted fur holds the evaporated sweat next to the skin, preventing it from escaping into the hot air of the environment and thus making the camel's sweating a far more efficient process than that of humans.

This efficiency extends even to urination. Most desert animals expend as little water as possible in urination. Where human urine must be about 95 percent water before it can be excreted, desert creatures need a far smaller percentage of water. If you follow the tracks of goats or ibex in the desert, walking along the line of dung pellets scattered over the hoofprints, you see white stains scattered here and there on the ground—the highly concentrated urine. The camel is one of the most meager urinators in the desert; its urine is four times as saline as that of humans, which means that it can thrive on very brackish water and on desert saltbushes. Even its feces contain hardly any water, which is why camel dung is the most common form of fuel in desert communities. The shiny black dung pellets are oblong, maybe two inches long, and very light. When you break them open, you find a light brown mass of coarse, almost dry plant fibers inside. The pellets burn slowly and evenly and without any odor.

The famous hump is also a specific design for desert

conditions. Like all animals, the camel carries its energy reserves in the form of fat, but unlike most, this fat is not distributed throughout the body but is concentrated in the hump. The size of the hump therefore changes according to feeding conditions. When a camel is freshly fed, its hump will be plump, firm, and upright. But after a long trek in the desert the hump has deflated; it is slack and shrunken, sometimes hardly even noticeable, for the animal has used up the entire energy reserve stored within it. There is a great deal of desert logic in the camel having all its fat on its back. Fat under its skin would hinder its ability to cool off in the desert night, but it needs a good solid layer of insulation on its back to come between it and the direct rays of the sun. Some researchers go further and claim that the camel produces water from the fat in its hump. In theory, about a pint of water would be produced for every pound of fat burned, since the metabolized fat produces hydrogen, which could combine with the oxygen that the camel breathes in, creating water. In practice, however, this is a very doubtful process since the camel breathes the extremely dry air of the desert, and if it were to take in sufficient oxygen to create water, it would lose more water than it created due to evaporation from its lungs.

Not only the hump, but the camel's whole shape is perfectly adapted to desert conditions. The peculiar lens shape of its trunk prevents the intense rays of the sun from striking it vertically, thus reducing their intensity. Its long legs raise it high enough off the ground to avoid the hotter air just above the sand, which reflects and radiates heat. And even the camel's behavior deflects the sun's intensity: never will you see a camel lying broadside into the sun. What you will see is the strange sight of whole herds of camels all sitting facing the same direction in the heat of midafternoon—backsides to the sun.

The quadruply jointed legs, the padded feet, the long neck, even the eyelids are all perfectly suited to the conditions in which the camel must live. It is the perfect desert animal, and as such, it has been invaluable to man. Without its extraordinary desert fitness, men could never have crossed the deserts of North Africa and the Middle East, let alone lived in them. Small wonder, then, that the camel has traditionally played such a vital role in Beduin life. Its milk has kept families and tribes alive for weeks when no other food or water was available, and Beduin going on a long journey will often take along a lactating camel. Its meat has been the occasion to honor a guest or to make peace. Its wool makes tents, carpets, rope, and saddlebags; its hide, thongs and leather trappings. Its dung serves as fuel, and even its urine is put to use: Beduin women may use it to rinse their hair, giving it the sheen they like, or it may be used medicinally, to pour on wounds as an antiseptic or even to drink for relief of stomach pain or diarrhea.

At a time when the explorers of the world were seaborne, the camel well deserved the title "ship of the desert." But for the Beduin it was far more than that; it was the very key to survival, and therefore a creature greatly prized. A man's wealth was estimated by the number of his camels, as was his power, for the camels were not only the source of sustenance and transport, but also the mounts on which the Beduin would raid caravans and wage their internecine wars. On a camel, a man can be independent in the desert. He can carry rations enough with him to see him through days alone far from wells or human settlement: flour and water, he need carry no more.

The preeminence of the camel in Beduin life is reflected in Beduin poetry, the oral history and culture of the desert people. Poetry for the Beduin is not the refined art it is in the West, but far closer to the troubadour style of the Middle Ages. Traditionally, it is sung to the mournful tones of the one-stringed violin, the *rabaaba*, as people gather around the campfire. It is a source of entertainment and education and an essential part of any festivity, but also, on a humbler and less heroic level, a casual way to mark an event in life, a feeling, a sorrow or a joy, generally intended only for a small group of intimates. There are no Beduin who consider themselves poets by profession. Poetry is part of their lives. And since the camel is an especially cherished part of their lives, it often appears in their poems. How important a part the camel plays is evident from the work of anthropologist Clinton Bailey, who has been collecting and translating Beduin poems and studying the culture and values expressed in them. The occasion for portrayals of camels, he writes, are poems sent as missives from one Beduin to another, usually written in rhyming couplets. "The message is entrusted to a cameleer who is charged with delivering it to the intended recipient. The poems often begin by describing the camel and go on to extol the virtues of the recipient. The poet displays his art by his skillful allusions to knowledge to which Beduin lay exclusive claim. Any Beduin worthy of the name should know, for example, that a camel which has just cut its canine teeth [at six years of age] is in its prime; that pedigree she-camels give little milk; and that a camel is considered thoroughbred when it is descended from five generations of acknowledged pedigrees." Thus:

> O rider upon one who has cut canine teeth,
> Whose hoofbeats on the broad plain inspire fear.
> Plundered by her herdsman from a thoroughbred herd
> No broker will take her to the *souk* for sale.
> She is sired by a male backed by six generations,
> Her mother's milk would not fill a cup.
> Her foreleg is lithe, her thigh is taut,
> And her waist as slim as the bow of a *rabaaba*.
> She carries saddlebags that shine, so fine is their wool,
> And a carbine that drops the most stubborn of wolves.

"This description serves not only to embellish the poem's message," writes Bailey, "but to win the listener's favor. It is a compliment to the recipient, as if the poet were saying: 'You deserve to receive messages on camels such as these.' By contrast, however, if a poet wants to insult the intended recipient, he 'sends' him a jaded beast." Anayz, a famous smuggler presently considered to be the best poet in the Sinai, once sent the following poem as a warning to Beduin who had not yet paid him for a smuggled shipment of hashish:

> O rider, riding on an exhausted mount
> Who can scarcely hold a blanket and her saddlebag,
> A black-skinned, scabby and tattered nag
> Whose whole life is spent in going around;
> Who commences her mission as a wolf in the hills
> Cowers beneath the pop of a hunter's shot.

But Anayz belongs to a dying culture. In the last generation or so, the jeep has fast been replacing the camel throughout the deserts of the Middle East. The transistor radio now provides more varied entertainment than the *rabaaba* and the poem. The nomadic life of the Beduin of the Middle East has practically halted altogether, and Beduin are working in towns and settlements, cooperating with the authorities, sometimes voluntarily, sometimes because there is no other alternative. Slowly but surely they are settling into modern mass culture. In the process, they are losing their values and way of life, their beliefs, and their culture. "Many Beduin under forty consider their ancestors' singular form of aesthetic expression foreign to their own experience," says Bailey, "and as the older generation dies off, the poetry, as well as other oral traditions, may disappear." In fact it *is* disappearing, fast, as Bailey recently found out when a famed octogenarian, one of the leading story- and poem-tellers of the Sinai, died four days before Bailey was due to meet him, taking with him his rich collection of tales and songs.

As the Beduin tradition fades, so does the importance and value of the camel. We now face the possibility that this superbly designed creature, without whom men could never have survived in the desert, may become "redundant," a mere appendix hanging on the artificial intestines of new roads and telegraph wires stretching across the desert. The camel cannot adapt, but the Beduin can and are doing so. As government efforts to settle them permanently intensify throughout the Middle East, as their sons go off to seek the "good life" of the towns, as pilgrims on the annual *hadj* to Mecca crowd into buses instead of taking the once-famed camel caravan south-ward from Damascus, the Beduin are painfully aware that time is rapidly passing them by and that their adaptation threatens their identity. Here is one poem composed in the 1930s, when many Beduin switched to goatherding because goat butter, oil, and sour milk could bring them a better income than camel breeding at a time when the wheel was encroaching on the desert:

> Raise the ship of the desert with her coarse hocks
> And don't let your head be turned by butter.
> Goatherds get gray long before their time
> From fear of the wolf they must fetter their flocks.
> But the camel, by contrast, drives all worry out
> And her milk will sustain you even in drought.

It is not only the camel that is in peril, but the whole Beduin way of life.

7 · Lore

Suleiman made music as he ground the coffee. He had already roasted the beans over a small fire of camel-dung pellets glowing softly in the sand, and now he was pounding the beans to a fine grain. The metal of the pestle met that of the mortar in a seductive, syncopated rhythm, so that all those gathered around beat their hands on their thighs or swayed in time to the grinding coffee. He used the sides and base of both pestle and mortar to beat out his tempo, easing the task of his pounding with the music in his implements. The music lifted suddenly into a higher, quicker rhythm, and then wafted down again into the solid dance of his basic theme. As the others talked and automatically moved hands and bodies, Suleiman half closed his eyes, the desert version of a jazz drummer into his set. Another Beduin brought out his flute, a reedless piece of metal piping with holes punched low down on one side. Its sound was that of the wind howling over the dunes in a storm; but the flutist couldn't match Suleiman's virtuosity, and Suleiman, knowing this, grinned wickedly as he changed into yet another rhythm. The flutist shrugged with a helpless smile and put his flute to one side.

In ten minutes, the coffee was ground. Suleiman threw it into a *finjan*, an ornate narrow-necked coffeepot, together with a generous measure of cardamom seeds, called *hell* in Arabic. He placed the *finjan* on the dung fire, and when the boiling liquid rose up in bubbles that raised the lid, he lifted it off the fire with his bare hands and poured the coffee into tiny white enamel cups traced with delicate blue patterns.

It was bitter as sin. And strong. And as the sun rose higher into the early-morning sky over the sand dunes of the northern Sinai, it brought us all wide awake.

We were some half-dozen people, but our number kept changing. For besides myself and "Capitan Ibrahim," the Beduin nickname for Captain Avi of the Israel Defense Forces, who was the Northern Sinai Command's liaison officer to the Beduin—a young man with a luxuriant but well-trimmed moustache who bore a striking resemblance, despite the fact that he was Israeli, to Egyptian film star Omar Sharif—the rest of our number were Beduin trackers working for the Israeli army. Some had just finished a night patrol and came to sit and unwind a little before sleeping. Some had just woken and were readying for a daytime patrol. Others were not on patrol at all that day and were delighted at the opportunity to entertain a guest with tracking tales.

Around us, the day's activity had begun. It was late summer, and the date palms stretching in a loose straggling line westward from El Arish halfway to Ismailia were heavy with huge bunches of deep red fruit hanging against the deepening blue of the sky, the dates defying gravity and begging to be harvested. These palms and the fish in the Mediterranean a few miles to the north are why most of the twenty-five thousand Sinai Beduin concentrate in this part of the peninsula. The younger men and the boys were off either working in the Gaza Strip or sitting in the coffeehouse of the Bir el-Abed village some miles away exchanging news and settling the politics of their everyday lives. Harvesting the dates is an old man's task, and a hard one.

One old man approached a tall, straight palm nearby. He wore wide baggy pants, tapering into the calf, and had tucked his cloak into his waistband. Around his waist he'd wrapped a thick rope. Now he slung the end of the rope around the trunk of the tree and tied it into his waist, so that man and tree were bound into the same circle of rope. He slung the rope upward on the far side of the palm's trunk, and leaning backward, hauled himself up after it. Balancing against the tree with his feet, he suddenly leaned inward to create a slack and again threw the rope up on the tree trunk, heaving his body up after it, until he finally reached the sharp palm fronds twenty feet off the ground and the huge nuggets of red fruit hanging beneath them. These he cut one by one with a large knife, attaching them to his waistband until, heavy with fruit, he slowly began his descent, man and tree still bound together within the circle of rope. Below the tree, his wives, daughters, and granddaughters were hauling large sacks, stuffing them with rotten or green dates that had fallen to the ground. These would be used for goat fodder, since in traditional Beduin life nothing goes to waste. Some of the men cut off the less healthy branches of their palms—for each harvests his own palms, and all recognize which palms are whose. Later that day, they would take the branches into El Arish and sell them to Jews coming south in search of palm branches for their *sukkot*, the open reed huts in which religious Jews eat during the eight days of the autumn harvest festival. The Beduin regard this Jewish custom with a certain amount of ironic humor; after all, in this part of the Sinai, most of them live the year round in palm-branch huts.

The trackers watched, sometimes chatting with the old man and offering advice, receiving for their pains presents of the ripest freshly picked dates, plump and juicy inside their thin brown skins. "Capitan Ibrahim" left; he had to be in the United Nations buffer zone, between where we were sitting and Egypt, to supervise a "population transfer," mainly students from Gaza going to Cairo to resume their studies. Juammar, the chief tracker, had agreed to initiate me into the secrets of his art.

A tall, gentle man in his late thirties, with deep-set soft black eyes and a high forehead creased with worry lines, Juammar was the best of the trackers in this part of the desert. In one day he could show me most of the basics, he said, and if I worked at it, I could probably become a reasonably competent tracker within three months. But, he said, asking my age, to be a really good tracker I'd have to have started thirty-three years ago. . . .

The Israeli army employs Beduin trackers because, as Juammar pointed out, they were born into the art. Most of the trackers here were from tracking families. Their fathers had been trackers, and their fathers' fathers before them. For in the desert, men are always wary of groups of other men. Beduin tribe has fought Beduin tribe, Beduin have fought the settled population on the fringes of the desert, and nation has fought nation. It has always been important to be able to read the tracks of other men in the desert, to know where they were and what they were doing. But since February 1976, when the Sinai interim agreement between Israel and Egypt came into effect, establishing the United Nations buffer zone in a wide swathe arching up from the Suez Canal, the army trackers had been concerned less with Egyptian infiltrators than with Beduin smugglers.

The trackers were mainly from the Negev, not the Sinai, so that they would feel no conflict of interest in helping catch Sinai Beduin transgressing Israeli law. Since 1967, when Israel conquered the West Bank of the Jordan River in the Six-Day War, the Negev Beduin have done very little smuggling; the direct and legal access of West Bankers to Jordan over the Jordan River took their trade away from them. But in the northern Sinai, over 80 percent of the Beduin's income still comes from smuggling, for the Beduin live off whatever the desert offers, whether it be natural or political. This is their place—their very name comes from *badiya*, the Arabic for desert. It is theirs in the sense not of possession, but of being an integral part of it. If outsiders establish new laws, foreign laws, in the desert, then the Beduin will either fight them or superficially acquiesce, whichever seems expedient, and use them, if they can, to their own advantage.

Smuggling has long been an honorable occupation among the Beduin, combining as it does their traditional disdain for outside authority with the art of exploiting whatever political situation prevails. In this, I sympathize entirely with the smugglers, partly because of my English upbringing, in which the pirates and smugglers of old were imbued with a romantic haze that allayed moral judgment; partly because I see nothing intrinsically wrong in the traffic of tape recorders, hashish, silk, and tea; and partly because I too see the desert as a place inherently beyond human political control. So that, as I set out with Juammar and three others to get my first introduction to tracking, all my questions were put from the point of view of the smuggler—how to avoid being caught—rather than from that of the tracker. It was to be a very frustrating introduction to smuggling.

At one point, we came across the tracks of three people in the sand. "You see," said Juammar, squatting down by the tracks. "Here, a woman and a girl passed some hours ago. And here," pointing to larger prints, "a man passed, maybe half an hour ago."

"How can you tell what sexes these people were?"

"Women walk differently from men. They spread their weight differently; their paces are shorter and they have smaller footprints."

"But how do you know who passed when, that they didn't all come here together?"

"Look well. You see, the tracks of the woman and the girl are less clear than the third set. They're a bit blurred, because since they were made, there's been a breeze, and the sand has drifted a little. The man's tracks are sharper. Also, he was going a lot faster than the woman and the girl."

"How do you know that?"

"You can see by the depth of each print. Look," he said, getting up to pace the sand around him. "If I walk slowly, my prints are this deep at the heels and this deep at the toes. But if I walk fast," picking up pace, "then my toes dig in deeper. And if I run," he said, beginning to sprint, "then my toes dig in really deep, and you can hardly see my heels. Try it."

I did, and backtracked to find my every action clearly imprinted on the sand behind me. It was a strange feeling. I was extremely conscious of my feet, aware of the fact that I could never be separated from them and that they, my contact with the ground, would inform whoever could see not only that I had been there, but also when, and what I had been doing.

"Okay," I said, "but if I knew I was likely to be tracked and wanted to avoid you, then couldn't I put sheepskins on my feet to blur the tracks, and then join older tracks to fool you into thinking that three people had passed a few hours ago, instead of two then and myself only recently?"

Juammar looked impressed by my knowledge—picked up earlier in the morning from one of the tracking tales told over the coffee—but shook his head almost sadly. "No, that wouldn't work. Your tracks would always be on top of the others. You see," he said, squatting down to the sand again, "the tracks of the woman and the girl cross every now and again. You can see where. Sometimes the woman crossed the path of the girl; sometimes the girl crossed over to the other side of the woman. But the man's tracks are always on top. His tracks cross theirs but theirs never cross his. This is the only way it can be, because he was here later, not with them. So if you used a sheepskin, I'd still see that you were here later because your tracks would be the top ones. And from that I'd know that you were deliberately trying to conceal your tracks, and that would make me really suspicious."

I racked my brains for an alternative. Juammar stood by patiently as I looked at the prints of my boots and then took them off, walking barefoot in the hot sand. The difference between the two sets of prints was clear, yet in both, there were the clear signs of a woman walking. Then I hit on a solution. If I could jump far enough, I might be able to tread only on the bushes that grew here and there on the dunes. They were barely a few inches high for the most part, but were generally more than a foot's span in width. I tried, and failed. They were too far apart, and I kept falling into the sand.

"But maybe someone who trained for it could manage it?" I queried hopefully.

Juammar looked even sadder. "Jump onto that bush there," he said. "In fact, no, don't jump, just walk on it." I did so. Juammar leaned over the bush and showed me where the weight of my step had broken the twigs of the bush.

"But there must be some kind of bush that doesn't break," I tried.

"There is," said Juammar, and he showed me a tiny gray-green plant. I stepped on it, and its leaves and twigs sprang up again resiliently. I was delighted, until I looked around and saw that it was the rarest of the dune plants. There was one, perhaps, every twenty yards or so.

"Well, what if despite all this I still managed to lose you. What would you do then?"

"I'd take a circle from the place where I lost you. I'd move out to a radius of a hundred yards, maybe more, depending on where we were and when, and then I'd gradually spiral inward on you. That way, even if you'd made for a palm grove where you could jump from tree to tree and leave no tracks, I'd close in on you."

"But surely it's impossible to leap around a palm grove like that," I exclaimed, thinking of the sharp points on the palm trunks and fronds and the distance from one tree to another.

"Nothing's impossible when you're desperate," said Juammar ominously, with more feeling than I might have expected from the hunter for the hunted.

"I could always bury whatever I was carrying in the sand," I offered, feeling rather desperate myself by now. "Then if you did catch up with me I'd at least be empty-handed."

"We'd find it," said Juammar, shaking his head again. And to prove his point, he disappeared over the dunes for a while and came back telling us to follow his tracks. Slowly, we set off, with Juammar questioning us every now and again as to what he'd been doing. Under his guidance, we saw where he'd gone slowly, where he'd run, where he'd tried to jump from bush to bush, where he'd backtracked to try and throw us off, where he'd walked in other tracks. And then we found a place where he'd stopped and squatted down. It was by a bush. The sand beside the bush was undisturbed. We thought no more of it and went on. Juammar stopped us with a sharp shout. He was willing to forgive me, but not the other trackers. "What about the other side of the bush?" he shouted. "Why should I bury something this side of it if I know I'm being followed? I used my head; now use yours!" And sure enough, the sand on the far side of the bush was disturbed. Juammar had leaned over the bush to bury a tin can among the roots on the far side of it, and we'd missed the deep print of his toes, which should have told us that he'd leaned over.

By now I was becoming convinced that a smuggler who knows that a good tracker is after him might just as well give up. The only reason smuggling was so successful, I reflected, was that there were just not enough trackers—only a dozen in this area—and the law of averages said that the smuggler would successfully complete his mission most, but not all of the time. A tracker like Juammar could tell my sex and, roughly, my age from my tracks. He could tell when I had passed and whether I was walking slowly or hurrying—any sign of hurry always being a reason for suspicion in this part of the world. If I was going straight, that in itself would be suspicious, since most Beduin walk along the curved sides of the dunes in order to keep as much on a level as possible, thus conserving energy though walking a longer distance. If I tried walking backward to deceive my trackers, I would leave very different prints from those of walking forward, since the deep parts of the print would suddenly be at the heel instead of the toe and the paces would be distributed differently. I couldn't combine my tracks with others already on the ground, even if they were fresh, since my tracks would always be on top. Juammar could reconstruct my every action along the trail—

where I had stopped, where bent down, where looked around—and could even tell if I was carrying a heavy burden. He would know if I were anxious to avoid detection, and, since he could tell all this from a moving jeep or even from the height of a camel, he would catch up with me very rapidly. And of course there was no way to wipe out my tracks; I had only to take a branch and try to do so for just a few seconds to see that the mess I was making with the branch was even easier to follow than my footprints.

"I guess there's no way to avoid a tracker who's after you," I mused, and Juammar sagely nodded. I remembered the amazement of Butch Cassidy and the Sundance Kid when an Indian tracker followed them everywhere, despite every avoidance trick they could think of. I told Juammar about the movie, laughing. It was all so clear now. At one point, Cassidy jumps from his horse onto that of his friend, and the two of them head off on one horse in a different direction from the riderless horse, thinking at least to confuse their followers. But now even I could see through that one. The heavier weight on the horse with two riders and the lighter weight on the riderless horse would be clear from the tracks. In fact, one could tell exactly where the leap from horse to horse had taken place, since the effort of the leap itself would drive the hoofprints farther into the ground. I could also see how the two cowboys had been tracked over the rocks, though I knew that it would take years of training for me to be able to do that. Even on the rocks there would be dust slurs and broken twigs where a horse had passed. There is no such thing as absolutely clean rock, and an experienced tracker could follow tracks over rock almost as fast as he could over sand. The magic of the tracking in the movie had become both an art and a science thanks to Juammar, and I marveled at how the two cowboys knew so little of Indian lore that they could not understand how the tracker was following them.

Armed with my introductory knowledge of tracking, I now tried to draw up a short list of smuggler's tips. It was a very short list indeed: it had only three points on it. But for what they are worth to any potential desert smuggler, they were as follows: (1) Always move slowly, and never in a straight line, so that your movement approximates as closely as possible the movements of innocent people in the area. (2) Place sheepskins over your feet, woolly side out (other animal skins will also do, but sheepskins are best), to blur your tracks, so that at least the time of your passing will be disguised. (3) Travel in a sandstorm . . . and take a compass.

This last method, it seemed to me, is the only one that is foolproof, since the wind and flying sand would cover your tracks within a couple of seconds. Anyone, I thought, who would be willing to walk or ride for hours through a sandstorm in dunes such as these would deserve to avoid capture. I put it to Juammar. "Excuse me, but for that you'd have to be crazy," he said.

By early afternoon, when we returned to Suleiman and the little dung fire, I was haunted by the idea of my tracks, feeling impossibly earthbound. Everywhere I went, my tracks followed me. I felt like a child trying to escape my shadow, remembering doing the strangest contortions in order to do just that (I had read a fairy tale in which someone had lost his shadow in Faustian style). Now here I was, an adult, doing basically the same thing . . . and enjoying it just as much.

Suleiman greeted us with another dance rhythm pounded out on his pestle and mortar. As the coffee boiled in the *finjan*, he produced a huge bowl of dates and brought out a large blackened teakettle. While Juammar emphasized the lessons of the day, we sipped a tiny cup of coffee, then three or four glasses of sweet tea, followed by more coffee, and more tea. Where the coffee was bitter and sharp, the tea was like a hot sweet liqueur, for Suleiman had poured as much sugar as tea into the kettle before placing it on the fire to boil.

This sweet tea is a relatively new custom. A hundred years ago, the Beduin of this area were drinking coffee, introduced to it, perhaps, by the Turks, but they knew nothing of tea. It may have been the British who introduced the weed when they took over the Sinai formally in 1906, or it may have been somewhat earlier; no one knows for sure. And although today it seems an integral part of the Beduin life-style, for some Beduin it has been near-disastrous—not because of the tea itself, but because of the vast amounts of sugar drunk in it. In Ein Gedeirat, for example, the luscious oasis in the center of the northern Sinai known also as Kadesh Barnea or Ein Gadis, the Beduin have mortgaged their livelihood for the sake of sugar in their tea. Like most of the northern Sinai Beduin, they are semi-settled, and their tents at the oasis serve as their main base the year round. They seem to lead an idyllic life, growing corn, wheat, pomegranates, dates, and many other fruits and vegetables and relaxedly eating whatever is in season—good living indeed by Beduin standards. When one frustrated Israeli researcher asked why they didn't store produce so that they would have a varied menu the year round, she was answered by "What for? There's always something to eat, thanks be to Allah." And when she asked why they didn't market their produce instead of giving away what was left over, the reply was "Who would want to buy? And why take the trouble to go to market? We have more than enough for our needs."

Perhaps it was this easygoing approach that led the Gedeirat Beduin into bankruptcy. At all events, by the 1920s many of them were no longer the owners of the land they farmed around the plentiful spring of Ein Gedeirat. For they had started to drink tea and were heavily in debt to the sugar merchants of El Arish, over fifty miles away to the northwest—so heavily in debt that the El Arish merchants assumed title to half the Beduin lands around the spring. The arrangement was that the Beduin would still live there and farm the land but would put aside a certain proportion of each year's produce for the new El Arish owners. They were not giving away their leftover produce, but paying their due tithe to their "sugar lords."

But such concerns were far from the minds of the army trackers. They were discussing their paychecks, oblivious to the price of sugar because though they had taken good care to buy their own tea—a finely crushed and very strong Gaza brand called Cleopatra—they used the army stores of sugar. As the heat of the day grew heavy on us, Suleiman traced what looked like a chessboard into the sand with a finger and challenged another of the trackers to a game. Suleiman gathered sixteen small black pellets of camel dung, his opponent searched out sixteen white pebbles, and they began to play a game very similar to the Japanese go, a game of territory and confiscation of the opponent's pieces when surrounded, to the tune of plentiful advice, good and bad, from the onlookers.

By the time I was finally getting the hang of the game, Captain Avi, alias Capitan Ibrahim, drove up in his jeep, back from the buffer zone. An Arabist, this Israeli-born son of Yemenite immigrants perfected his Arabic working with Beduin trackers in the Negev in the mid-sixties. He seemed young for his job—seven months younger than I—but his reputation throughout the area, among both the Israeli forces and the Beduin, was very high. Now he jumped out of the jeep looking as though he were just in from a long rest rather than a day spent in the heat of the sun processing travelers through the buffer zone. His immense shock of black hair, shot here and there with a streak of white, was immaculate, and his smile under the well-trimmed moustache easy and fresh. He joined in the game, replacing the losing player, and won, and then picked up the metal flute and played a perfect Beduin melody on it.

"How come you play better than the man the flute belongs to?" I asked.

"I should," replied Avi. "After all, I taught him how to play the flute in the first place."

An Israeli army liaison officer teaching Beduin how to play their own folk tunes? "Yes, and poems too. I've been collecting Beduin songs from the elders. The younger people hardly know them, and it hurts to see a culture dying out like that. So I try to keep it alive a little by passing on what I know." It was hardly the classical romantic picture of the proud Beduin jealously guarding his lore to himself, but it had the tangible credibility of reality, of the absurdities and paradoxes of the desert in the twentieth century.

I took my leave of Juammar, Suleiman, and the others, with detailed instructions on how to find their tents in the northern Negev covering pages of my notebook, and set off with Avi to visit a tribal headman a few miles away. This man was not the sheikh of the tribe, Avi explained, but the power behind the sheikh. For the last hundred years or so, he said, many of the tribes, aware that a sheikh may be seduced by promises of money or influence from outside authorities, have appointed the man best at buttering up the authorities as their sheikh, assuring their independence meanwhile by maintaining the identity of the true strong man of the tribe a secret from outsiders. Since his identity, and usually even his existence, is unknown to the authorities, his loyalties cannot be turned from the tribe. But like so much of traditional Beduin life, this system too is breaking down, for Captain Avi of the Israeli military administration knew who the true tribal headman was—and the headman knew that Avi knew.

It was a slow journey, for everyone along the way knew Avi and wanted to say hello. We picked up a young teenager who told Avi his brother was out of jail, where he'd served a term for smuggling. "It's good it was you who caught him this time," said the boy. "There's more honor that way, and it made everything simpler."

"But it may not be me who catches him next time," said Avi, "so he'd really better stop smuggling."

"Ah well," sighed the boy, and shrugged with a disarming grin, knowing that smuggling was his brother's way of life.

Many brief stops later, just as the sun was setting, we reached a small encampment of reed huts set in a small plain among the dunes. Avi drove first to a hut in the middle of the encampment, searching out a young Beduin woman married less than a year ago, for whom he felt a certain responsibility. She had come to him as a disinterested outsider for advice on whom she should marry, the man she wanted or the man her father wanted her to marry, and Avi had intervened with the father to persuade him of her case. Behind her in the hut, a dark-skinned blond baby crawled in the dust. She held an infant in her arms and nodded and laughed delightedly like a child—she was only a teenager—as Avi asked how things were with her. When Avi commented on how quickly she had had children, she cocked her head to one side and winked. "Allah's will!" she said, raising her eyes skyward. Later Avi told me that she had once asked him about birth control, though she refused to divulge where she had even heard of such a thing. But she had evidently not yet visited the military administration's medical clinic in El Arish.

We didn't stop long with her, for Avi was overusing his privilege among the Beduin by stopping there at all. We drove on to the guest hut, situated slightly away from the rest of the village, and there the headman and a few others, having seen the jeep, were already waiting for us. The titular sheikh was away in El Arish. Avi introduced me, and we all shook hands. I was to be an honorary man for the purposes of this visit. A quilt was placed on the sand outside the hut for us—since Avi had insisted that this was not a formal visit, we did not go inside—and cushions were piled up on the quilt so that Avi and I sat to either side of a small wall of comfort, leaning on the cushions in the classical reclining posture with one leg drawn up and the other lying straight out. As our hosts started a fire in the sand and brought water, Avi explained the symbolism of the Beduin welcome.

Signs, omens, and symbols are a vital part of life in the desert. The Beduin use signs to convey to others of their tribe who a stranger is. A member of the tribe may bring a guest to the guest tent or hut. If he sits down beside the guest, then the man is a friend and welcome, but if he ushers the guest into the inner circle and himself sits down by the wall, then he has been coerced into bringing the guest, and the man is immediately suspect. Or if a Beduin walks into the guest tent or hut and does not know who a stranger is, he will sit in the outer circle until it becomes clear from the drift of the talk. If he cannot tell, he will stay in the outer circle, but if he knows the man for an enemy or as untrustworthy, he will walk out, thus signaling his knowledge to the others. Such are the ways that the Beduin deal with non-Beduin guests, ways that preserve their face in hospitality and also allow them to act without giving themselves away. The laws of the desert are observed; one does not turn away a stranger or refuse him drink, for these are part of the basics of human survival in the desert. But onto this basic fabric of hospitality, the Beduin have woven an intricate Gobelin of signs and signals.

Since so much leeway had already been accorded me in ignoring my sex and giving me a place as an honored guest in the circle of men now gathering around the fire, I asked if I might look inside the guest hut, for I was curious as to its design. Unlike the round living huts, it was squared off. The headman accompanied me, indicating a full black clay water jug lying in one corner, and an ornate *finjan* in the other. But my main interest was the huge wooden beam that ran the length of the hut. It had apparently once been the mast of a ship that had broken up in a storm at sea; the Beduin must have found it on the beach and brought it inland to this encampment, there to have it grace their guest hut. But when I asked when they found it, the headman just shook his head and smiled. "Many years ago," he said. The ceiling was made of palm fronds and reeds lying on large perforated iron sheets, which Avi later identified for me as the sheets used by the Egyptian army to get armor and other vehicles over very sandy terrain. The pillars at the corners of the hut were railroad sleepers, presumably from the long disused railroad that once ran down the eastern Mediterranean coast from

Beirut to Ismailia. In their architecture as in their customs, the Beduin had adapted and innovated, using the events and happenings around them not only to weave the fabric of their lives but also to build their homes.

We returned to the circle, I to my place on Avi's left and the headman to his place on Avi's right. The circle had grown larger meanwhile, and beside me sat a newcomer, introduced as the headman's brother. I tried not to stare, but still looked as much as I could without seeming to do so, for the brother could have been the twin of an Austrian-born *Time-Life* photographer in Jerusalem, David Rubinger. He had the same eyes, the same facial structure, same mouth, same voice, even, to my utter amazement, the same gestures and facial expressions. Again the absurdity of reality overcame me. To one side was the Jewish liaison officer who looked so much like Omar Sharif, and to the other, the Beduin who looked so much like the Jewish photographer. I tried to picture Rubinger in a kaffiyeh and long flowing jelebiyeh, or Sharif in the casual uniform of the Israeli army—absurd, yet quite possible. But I had evidently been staring after all, for now I felt the brother's eyes on me.

"It was you who bought cigarettes yesterday in Bir el-Abed, wasn't it?" he said.

I was stunned. Bir el-Abed was a tiny Beduin village some twenty miles away, and I had indeed bought cigarettes there early the morning before, stopping briefly at one of those packed Beduin stores that stocks everything from plastic sandals to tiny unlabeled vials of pungent sweet perfume. But this man had not been there, and I had said nothing in the store as to who I was. And forgetting for a moment that I was only an honorary man, and that an Israeli woman on her own in this part of the world was an event in itself, I asked how he knew. He just smiled broadly, raising his hand and narrowing his eyes in the universal gesture of "news travels."

Now that he had identified me, the headman's brother admired my watch, asking if it was real gold. I laughed. Not

only was it imitation, I said, but it was a cheap one that had
never let me down over fifteen years, for no matter how much
sand got into it, it always seemed to work. The headman
smiled at the story; he pulled out a beautiful fob watch from
inside his jelebiyeh and handed it over to me. It was a real
timepiece, with gold finishing, a gold chain, and Roman
numerals delicately printed on the face. Lettering on the face
proclaimed in English and Arabic that it had been made by a
firm based in London and Cairo. That watch, he said, as I
admired it, was twenty-five years old and going as well as the
first day he got it.

"That's from the good old days of smuggling, hm?" said
Avi, knowing that the headman was one of the most famous
smugglers in the area and that though he himself no longer
rode the smugglers' routes, he still organized others.

"Aiee-wa," sighed the headman, a long, drawn-out Arabic
yes that expressed worlds of past glories and present straits.
And Avi and he smiled sadly at each other.

As the tea was served, our host ordered supper for us,
sending a boy off to the living huts to tell the women to
prepare it. Turning back to us, he overrode Avi's protests by
indicating the evening star high over the horizon and telling
us, with a broad smile, that he had no choice but to feed us,
since as long as the evening star shone, he was bound by the
rules of hospitality to offer food to his guests.

Fascinated, I asked for more star stories, telling the next one
myself, as I remembered the time when, late at night on a high
mountain in the Negev, I had stood with arms outstretched so
that it had seemed that I was holding the Milky Way in my
palms, the magnificent mass of stars pouring in an arc over my
head from one hand into the other as though I were some
celestial juggler. It was a good story, said the headman, but it
would be still better if I were to call the Milky Way by its
Beduin name, the "Way of Dates"—a name that seemed to
make special sense at this time of year, with the millions of
dates hanging in demonstrative fertility from the palms.

I asked if he would tell us the story of the Plough, and he looked at me in surprise and sudden regard as I mentioned the story. Avi was even more surprised, for he had never heard of it, and the headman now told it slowly and in great detail, in the Beduin way. It was a beautiful tale of tragedy and suspense involving Polaris, the constant north star; Canopus, the south star that shines for only a couple of hours before dawn between October and May; and the stars of the Plough constellation. The four main stars of the Plough, as the tale goes, are the bier of a man who has been murdered by Polaris. The stars that form the shaft of the Plough are his four daughters, who weep bitterly as they carry his bier through the sky. They make their way toward Canopus, the south star, for they are convinced by Canopus's evasive behavior that he is the murderer, and they seek revenge to the south. Meanwhile Polaris, the true murderer, braves it out and flaunts Canopus, who never has time to prove his innocence. The Beduin name for the Plough is thus *Banat an-Na'ash*, "Daughters of the Bier," and whenever someone is unjustly accused of any crime, the legend comes alive in the Beduin proverb which translates, "While Polaris did the killing, Canopus is accused."

Sensing the warmth accorded me for my knowledge of the Plough story, I thought it a good time to explore something that had been haunting me for some months—the number forty, which seemed to gain larger proportions as a symbolic number special to the desert the more I thought about it. In the legends and religions that had arisen in these deserts of the Middle East, it seemed to occur everywhere. When it referred to time—to forty years of wandering or to forty solitary days and nights—it seemed to signify the desert as a place of spiritual cleansing and preparation for what was to come. But it occurred in other contexts as well, such as the Moslem legend that forty thousand prophets have arisen out of this desert since the beginning of time. And I knew that it was still alive today, in this very desert. I knew, for example, that the

Beduin call the cold winter spell *el-arbiniyah*, the forty days, and that a common Beduin cure for numerous maladies was *el-arbain*, the forty, a mixture of the saps of forty plant species mixed with olive oil and clarified butter. I had even been told of the belief of the coastal Beduin of the southern Sinai in the efficacy of the sea turtle's penis as a cure for impotence, since the sea turtle, it is said, mates for forty consecutive days every year. So now I seized the opportunity to ask for more instances of forty.

At first, the examples came hesitantly from around the circle, one by one. But within a short time, they were flooding out, so that I quickly asked leave to jot them down in my notebook. Within forty paces of his home, or of the home of a man who gives him shelter, a man cannot be attacked, no matter how strong the cause. Forty days is the appointed period of mourning. It takes forty days for a broken bone to mend. A woman is forbidden to have intercourse with her husband for forty days after childbirth, and for that same period must wear gold to protect her against the evil spirits emanating from menstruating women around her. The quail-hunting season here in the northern Sinai lasts forty days (as the quail fly south from Europe to Africa for the winter). Flies pester the flocks of sheep and goats for forty days at the beginning of the summer and forty days at the end of it. A man is given forty days grace in which to pay an overdue loan. . . .

But why? I asked. Why forty instead of any other number, instead of thirty or fifty? Where does it come from?

But to that there was no answer, or not the one I sought.

"We don't know," said the headman finally, shaking his head in slow amazement. "Forty just seems to be everywhere; it's always been there, but there's no knowing why. It just is that way." And I was left with the number forty a still larger question in my mind, glowing with an undefined magical significance. There was no explanation, but simply a number that for some reason hidden within itself gained a special meaning in this very place, this desert, and no other.

And now the food arrived, brought over by the boys from the women in the living huts. Avi and I ate, and the headman and his brother joined us with a morsel here and there, for although they had eaten before sundown, hospitality demanded that they at least taste the food with us. There were large sand-brown *pittot*—unleavened bread baked over a fire on a rounded shield—and a dip of tomatoes and onions in olive oil, which we gathered up in the *pittot* and stuffed into our mouths, followed by the largest, sweetest olives I had ever eaten, each the size of a small crab apple, wrinkled and green. And with it all, of course, more tea. Thus we sat and ate and drank and talked some more until, the evening star long set behind the horizon, the visitors took their leave, and the hosts returned to their huts to sleep on the sand floor of the desert.

8 · Rock

Nothing, it seems, can be quite so inanimate as stone. Stonehearted, stone-deaf, stone-dead—the image of stone as impenetrable silence is set deep within our language, and through language, in our thinking. Yet something in the human psyche refuses to accept the awesome inhumanity of stone. The ancients worshiped stones, convinced that this inhumanity was suprahuman. Moses struck water from a stone, bringing forth from the inanimate the very stuff of life. The alchemists of the Middle Ages pondered the philosophers' stone and sought the secret of its transformation. Even today, in our own strange commercial ways, we seek to find life in stones, whether in such gimmicky ways as the Pet Rock craze that hit the United States some years ago or in the majestic obelisks that represented alien intelligence in Stanley Kubrick's film *2001*. Many of us have picked up a stone—on a beach usually—and pocketed it fondly perhaps because it reminded us of something: of a bird or a fish or any living thing. But it is a far step from seeing lifelike forms in one stone to seeing life in vast expanses of rock. Our imagination often leaps no further than a single stone, and it tends to turn away in dismay when confronted with the vast rock expanses of the desert.

The Sinai and Negev is mostly a desert of rock. This is what 70 percent of the world's deserts are made of: not the dramatic dunes of romance rolling sensuously into the distance, but the gaunt, naked crust of the earth laid bare to eyes and feet. It is harsh and uncompromising, with none of the curves and smoothness that we seek to lull our senses. But if you are lured as I am by this desert harshness, then inevitably you become caught up in the study of stone and rock, and you find out about synclines, exfoliation, faults, metamorphosis.

Yes, rocks metamorphose. Granite changes to gneiss, limestone to marble, and sandstone to schist as the pressure and heat of the multiple changes in the earth's crust intensify and lessen. Rock is animate. It bends and folds, folds and refolds to create valleys and mountains and then again valleys where once there were mountains, and mountains where once there was sea. Rock changes as we watch, but on a time scale so utterly different from ours that we see only absolute stillness and we speak, thinking it true, of "unchanging rock."

I first grasped the scale of this change on a midsummer field trip into the Ramon Crater, a twenty-five-mile-long scoop into the earth's crust in the very center of the Negev. For three days, the yellows and browns of the crater gradually worked their way into our eyes, staining the whites of them the color of the rock around us. On the morning of the second day, we raced up a hill of gypsum, our feet plowing through the thin crust to leave deep holes at each step. On top of this hill was a lacolite layer, and then another gypsum hill on top of that, said Amir, a young geologist. I reached the top first, eager to see. The lacolite lay on the surface, small sharp black stones reflecting the sun's brilliance in all directions. The others came up behind me, and I swung round in disappointment. "But there's no hill on top of this one," I protested. "This is the top!" Amir just smiled and said nothing.

Exasperated, I looked around me at the walls of the crater, the relentless blue of the sky, the reds, yellows, browns, and blacks of the crater floor. A hundred yards or so to the north was another hill of gypsum, slightly lower than the one on which we stood. I gazed. And laughed with realization. That was it: that hill over there was on top of this one, geologically speaking. At one time, it had stood right over this one, layer on layer of gypsum separated by lacolite. And then slowly, gradually, it had slipped down to the north as the whole crust of the earth moved.

Suddenly, the crater changed meaning for me. No longer was it a jumble of rocks and hills, colors and textures, but a fascinating whole, a clear picture of geological processes over a time span that I can state as hundreds of millions of years but never truly grasp. And yet here I could see those hundreds of millions of years unfolded before me—the time scale of geology.

The problem is that this scale is inhuman; it is beyond the grasp of the human mind. We can comprehend it intellectually but must also admit that it makes little difference whether we talk of rocks one million years old or a hundred million years old; we cannot envision even one million. Even those who have worked intensively with such numbers cannot do so. David Fayman, for instance, is an ex-physicist who works at the Desert Research Institute in Sde Boker. His prophetic mane of unkempt hair, his wild beard, and his thick glasses create the image of the mad physicist. He worked for a decade in particle physics, pondering the behavior of the quark, a particle whose existence is by definition unprovable, until, alarmed by the unworldliness of his theorizing and by the terrifying worldliness of the possibility of a quark bomb, he abandoned the field for the warmer and more earthy one of solar energy. Today, he is still fascinated by the fact that he can never see 10^6—a million. He fumes at the fact that millimeter graph paper is not produced in sufficiently large sheets for him to hang one square meter of it above his desk. That way, he says, at least he could see a million of something, even if only a million square holes. "Imagine, just to be able to see, grasp, and contemplate a million of something! The pity is that you can't take it further, can't see 10^{12}—a billion of something. That would be a square kilometer of millimeter graph paper, and even if you had it, you wouldn't be able to see it, because you'd have to go up in a helicopter to see the whole square kilometer, and then you wouldn't be able to make out the millimeter squares." His fantasy leaves me with the indelible image of Fayman and conceptual artist Joshua Neustein crawling over a square kilometer of graph paper laid out over the Negev hills. But Neustein, alas, is in the concrete pastures of New York, so that my image, in true conceptual art style, will remain just that and no more.

Fayman's complaint is that though we use such figures as a million and a billion all the time, we cannot grasp them. Our minds glaze over, and we reduce the irreducible to human size, imagining that quarks are real when they are mere figments of the human imagination. In the same way, we imagine that rock is solid, unmoving, merely part of the background to human existence. We exaggerate in order to keep track with our own existence, and in so doing we reduce things to the limits of our own comprehension. Take the globe, for instance—an expensive one made in relief. Swing it around, and you can feel the heights of the mountains and the depths of the valleys and ocean rifts moving beneath your fingers. But we have exaggerated enormously in order to comprehend, and our exaggeration has befuddled our comprehension. If such a globe were in true scale, the mountains and valleys of the earth, from the highest to the lowest, would be no more than the dust and scratches on a billiard ball, since that is the true dimension of the earth's crust in relation to the whole planet. The globe magnifies the importance of our own perceptions and thus of our own existence.

David Brower, America's archconservationist, put things into their true perspective when he compared the 4.6 billion years of the earth's existence to the six biblical days of Genesis. On this scale, he calculated, human beings appeared on earth only three minutes before midnight of the last day and Christ was born only a quarter of a second before midnight.

But even this is still only an intellectual perspective. The intellect can grasp the scale of time and space in the desert by talking of billiard balls and six-day weeks. But it still remains a scale that has nothing to do with man's existence or with the human sense of time and space. Is it even possible to see the time and space of the desert, and by seeing it to love it in the same way that we love the plants in our gardens, the trees outside our windows, the forests and meadowlands through which we walk on Sundays to breathe in the fresh air of what we know as nature? For what is natural to us is what we comprehend. You may have planted those flowers in your garden. If not you, then maybe your parents, or even your grandparents, or others no more than two or three generations back. Plants live on a human time scale. We can see them growing as we tend to them, and so we can love them. They grow as we do; often, they die before we do. Through them, we outlive nature and rise above it. And because the flowers, plants, and trees are soft and curved, live and die, we see them as beautiful.

But the desert? When I look at landscape photographs of the desert, I see monotony. I see jagged mountains, gaunt rocks, a landscape that looks inhuman and therefore repels me. Aesthetically I see no beauty in the desert. Often, it is extremely ugly. For the desert is beyond the perception of the camera or the workings of the eye. It is beyond aesthetics, and its power beyond beauty. It speaks to everything behind the eye, not to the eye itself. While the beauty of a coast or alpine mountains or pastoral hills is easily accessible and can be seen immediately, the beauty of the desert comes only to the eye of the person who loves it. And this love grows not out of seeing the desert, but out of being in it—finding out about it and becoming, in a sense, part of it. In the desert, vision comes from experience.

There is no vision of the moment, no instantaneous grasp such as that of the camera. I have never carried a camera in the desert, but occasionally a companion has taken one along. The resulting photographs would tell you much about my companions and myself, but little about the desert. There is Tsur's photograph of a large agama lizard, for example, taken among the ruins of a Byzantine monastery on Jebel Safsafa, the lower part of Mount Sinai. A small group of us had drunk water from a well there, and lain down to eat and rest a little in the shade of a large fig tree growing in the ruined courtyard. One by one, we fell asleep, each person finding a niche in which to shelter from the midafternoon sun. I slept under the tree, feet up on a stone and one arm flung over my face, to be awakened by a soft "ooh." Rising slowly, I opened my eyes to see a huge iguanalike agama on a ruined wall nearby, gazing at us all. It was a very deep turquoise blue. Tsur slowly reached for his camera and rose to a crouch; he raised the camera to his eye, adjusted the focus and then slowly, very slowly, began to creep closer to the lizard. We held our breaths, realizing that he did not see that as he inched closer to that exquisite blue creature, it was gradually changing color, fading into paleness. Now he must take the picture, we thought, now! But he didn't. He crept still closer. Two yards now, a yard and a half. And it became quite clear that he had forgotten the photograph, that, camera to eye, he simply wanted to get as close as possible to the agama, as though by hiding his face with the camera he were invisible to the creature, like a child who disappears by placing his hands over his eyes. It seemed to make no difference that the picture he wanted had already disappeared. The lizard, a faded nondescript gray by now, blended with the rock of the wall on which it perched. But Tsur crept closer still until, when he was within arm's reach, the agama quickly turned and disappeared, only the flash of its movement distinguishing it from the wall. That was the moment when Tsur finally clicked the shutter. Blinking, he lowered the camera and smiled happily at us. "How close was I?" he asked.

I was delighted. He had made an adventure of the act of photographing, knowing that the photograph itself was irrelevant and that this is the only way it can be in the desert, for the desert defies the frozen time of the camera's vision. Perhaps that is why I love the old etchings and sketches made by nineteenth-century travelers. They convey what the camera cannot, because they were created by people, not by technology, and the people drew what they felt more than what they saw. The mountains in old sketches of the Sinai are often out of scale, exaggerated, but the exaggeration is the true scale, far truer than the physical one. The sketches are true to the desert the traveler carries with him in his mind, for it is in the mind that the beauty of the desert exists. Not the "desert of the mind" that is used in popular speech to describe an empty desolation of mindlessness, but the rich expansiveness of the desert as it enters the soul. It is a beauty that is grasped not by the eyes but by the heart. Not just sight, but all five of the senses feed the growing feeling of desert until the desert finally demands, and receives, a commitment to it, an unshakable acknowledgment in the depths of one's soul of its beauty and its power.

The field-station people taught me this mode of seeing the desert. There are twenty-three field stations throughout Israel and the territories it controls, run by the Society for the Protection of Nature. Each station has about ten guides, all of them young and idealistic. Their main work is guiding groups of schoolchildren on organized outings, but there are many times in the year, especially in summer, when they are freed from their work to go out exploring on their own. Sde Boker is one of the best of these stations, with an extraordinarily warm and open bunch of people in it. The women all dress in what is practically regulation field-station style: very short shorts, a T-shirt or tank top, a kaffiyeh wrapped bandanna fashion around the head, two or three silver bangles on their wrists, and on their feet a well-worn dusty pair of *tanachiyot*, the ancient-style sandals whose Hebrew name translates as "biblicals." The men too wear short shorts and *tanachiyot*, and in summer that's it, though occasionally a very battered straw hat may be pulled out of the back of a jeep. Walking in the desert in *tanachiyot* is no easy matter, especially the way the field-station people walk. If they are guiding an organized trip, they will take the easy way, but once they are on their own, they'll go anywhere and do anything to see a bird, a stone, a flower, a lizard. Their rule, among themselves, is quite simply "straight up" or "straight over." And since straight up or over hot sand, thornbushes, or jagged mountains is hard on the ankles in *tanachiyot*, I stuck stubbornly to jeans and desert boots or sneakers throughout my time with them.

There is a cleanness about these dusty, slovenly dressed young people that is as refreshing as a dive into a wadi pool in the middle of a hot day, a freshness and clear-sightedness of vision through which shines the beauty of the desert. These people love the desert. To be in it with them is to share their joyful discovery of plants, creatures, rocks, the infinite variety and wisdom of the desert and its life. The head of the Sde Boker Field Station, Amir Edelman, is a geologist only a few years older than the guides whom he directs. He led us into the Ramon Crater for three midsummer days, infecting us all with his enthusiasm for rocks as he scribbled diagrams with a felt pen on the windshield of the jeep as we bounced over the wadi beds. He led us up and down, around and over, and finally, into the rock.

We had climbed halfway up the northern side of the crater, scrambling up a mass of shale that poured out of a hole in the crater wall. As we busily pried open segments of shale with our knives to find fossilized creatures inside, mainly scorpions, I wandered up closer to the hole, attracted by that open maw in the closed rock wall. I called the others up, and we peered anxiously into the hole, making out a tunnel that went straight into the mountain, its walls and roof a series of uneven rills. In width it was not much larger than a large man with arms outspread; in height, that large man would have had to stoop. "Let's go in," I said, and was instantly amazed by my own curiosity. When I am with the field-station people, I am usually the one who follows after. The crazy ideas are theirs, and I am the one led on into things that I would never normally do, like teetering on a two-inch ledge with a thousand-foot drop below me. But this time, after seeing, feeling, even tasting rocks and stones, I felt I had to get inside that rock in order to see it for what it was. The tunnel was enticing, with an alluring sense of the forbidden.

Five of us ventured into the dark maw, feeling our way along the curiously rilled walls as the tunnel curved away from the entrance to cut off all light. The floor was fairly regular, and soon we walked close together, side by side, advancing in a straight line into the darkness. As we went on, the air began to change. I had never known how air could be foul until then: it had a sharp acrid quality to it that hurt the throat and stung the eyes, fogging even the small degree to which the eyes could adjust to utter darkness. And then we saw a glimmer of orange: a bulb set into the wall of the tunnel, its light murky in the foul air, showing us the dimensions of the tunnel and the smokelike dust floating in the air. We passed again into darkness, and then reached another light, realizing now that the whole tunnel was lined with lights spaced at regular intervals, but that most of them were not working. The farther we went in, the less light each bulb seemed to cast, and the thicker the air became. By now, we were all holding hands. And then we came to a major fork in the tunnel. One branch went downward farther into the rock, a well-lit path with most of the lights working. The other, to the left, was entirely dark. But from it issued a heavy rumbling noise, as if some great creature was lurking in wait there. . . .

Perhaps we would not have been so scared nor had such associations had we not all seen a special viewing of the original *King Kong* film two days before. But now, in this murky darkness with the heavy growling rumbling up at us through the black tunnel, Kong was there, it seemed, waiting for us; so that we were quite prepared for the horror of seeing two bright beams suddenly shine out at us from deep down the tunnel as that grumbling increased in power to a roaring. Two round yellow beams of light reached toward us yet faded in the murkiness of the tunnel before they could catch us in their beams, and behind them was a flickering glow as though a huge fire were burning there, belching smoke and dust out past those beams of light into the tunnel, blinding our vision and filling our ears with that deep primeval roaring sound.

We were all caught in that curious suspension between knowledge of reality and the equally real knowledge of fantasy. We knew this was a shale mine and that somewhere there must be mining going on; but we knew, too, that Kong was a primordial creature, as primordial as this rock within which we had been moving. If any habitat in this part of the world could be his, then this was it. Again, something drew me on despite my usual trepidation. I stepped forward as the others huddled in conference; to my great relief, seeing me disappearing into the dark, they followed me. Where the tunnel floor had been fairly smooth until now, it became rough, full of potholes, and I kept blundering into them, even falling a couple of times. Now I began to be really frightened. The real knowledge was giving way fast to the fantasy knowledge, and I was stumbling into the maws of prehistory, into a place where no human should be. Those two round eyes of yellow light grew brighter, beadier as the sound increased in volume. The others caught up with me, and we held hands again, all quaking and trying unsuccessfully not to show it to the others. And then with the most enormous sense of relief I cried out: "Legs, I see legs!" I felt us all straighten up in relief; our pace quickened as we saw a man walking at the end of the tunnel, outlined by the fierce glow of light behind him.

Within a minute, we stumbled out into a small cavern aglow with arc lights, filled almost entirely by a huge machine some ten yards long and two yards wide. In front of it, facing toward the tunnel, was a pit truck, its full beams shining into the tunnel. The noise was awesome. As we crept around the machine, huddled against the cavern wall to avoid its sharp edges, we saw the source of the noise. It was like a giant machine gun except that instead of having a hollow barrel it was a solid revolving pole, with huge steel claws at the end that were biting into the shale rock, crisscrossing it as the barrel moved up and down, from side to side, eating out the shale and creating an ear-splitting complaint of steel on solid rock as it hit the top of the shale deposit again. My mind may have been tuned in to movies from having seen *King Kong*, or perhaps it was simply unavoidable for someone from our time and culture, but the image I saw was one of James Bond spread-eagled there against the shale as those giant steel claws reached for his flesh, with his archenemy astride the huge barrel of the machine laughing maniacally as the claws cut their way closer and closer to Bond's struggling body. . . .

There were three men around the machine, and though we tried to shout to them, they did not realize we were there until one of them turned and saw us. He was a huge burly man, with deep olive skin. He smiled broadly at us through the dust, and signaled to the others to cut off the machine. The silence was as loud as the drilling had been, and that, combined with the broad smiles and shining eyes of the three men watching us and that huge temporarily immobile claw, created an ineffable sense of evil. The name of the foreman was Zechariah. We asked him what they were mining the shale for. His teeth and eyes flashed as he threw his arms upward and roared out "Behemoth! This is food for Behemoth!" That ancient Hebrew word for primeval creatures, from his lips in this place, brought Kong stomping to the forefront of my mind again. Zechariah knew what he was doing; this was his mine, his territory, and he had brought out a word hardly used anymore in order to impress these wanderers from the world outside with the immensity of his work. He was the one who burst into rock; we, merely those who clambered over it, who knew the surface but not the innards of this vast ancient world beneath our feet.

The shale is used as a binder in animal feed, he finally told us, and also serves as a component in lubricating oils. But he was enjoying his status as an underground man too much to remain serious for long. I imagined him in his namesake's tomb in Jerusalem, that long semicircular underground tunnel inside the rock of the Mount of Olives with the graves of Zechariah and his followers in little pits leading off the main tunnel. How he would love that! Neither he nor his fellow workers wore pit helmets; neither did they have any oxygen masks down here, though the air intake from the surface was miserly. I asked why. "Who needs them?" he roared happily. "It's as good a place to die as any!" We turned to go, gasping for air by now. "Hey, the lights tend to go out," said Zechariah, "so if they do, just grab hold of the air pipe on the ground and follow it by feel. Don't try and remember your way out; there's ten kilometers of tunnel in this mountain, and you can get stuck down here for days." And so saying, with a paternal beam, he turned his back to us and started up the machine again. As we squeezed past it, I saw the make and brand of the drill embossed on the barrel: ALPINE MINER. In the middle of the desert.

The way back seemed short and easy now that the terrors of the tunnel had been made human. Amir and I were in the lead as we saw the light of open day at the end of the tunnel, and the two of us went running out, flinging our arms wide open, to stand stock still on the rock shelf outside the tunnel entrance whooping in delight. It was as though I were seeing the crater for the first time: the full shock of that marvelous huge open space before and above me, falling away below me in what minutes before had seemed an inconceivable expanse of space. For the first time, I felt the size of this crater, its depth and openness, its space and the quality of light in it. Its walls no longer seemed to close in on me; now, they towered with limpid curving grace toward the sky, reaching up powerfully into the blue.

Later, thinking about the terror and excitement of entering the mine and the joy of coming out of it, I could understand what makes people climb down into the earth's crust. It is the most direct way to find out what rock is, to contact the oldest part of the existence of this earth. It is not just touching but actually entering the stuff of which the earth is made. My intellectual picture of the tension and pressure of geotectonic forces over hundreds of millions, even billions of years had metamorphosed into a deep feeling for the tensile power of rock. In the mine I had been not just in the desert, but inside it; and in doing so, it seemed to me that I had been as close as humanly possible to the rock, to the primacy of the desert.

PART TWO

THE HUMAN
DESERT

9 · Conquering

Human beings are not desert creatures. The scarcity of water and the extremes of temperature in the desert demand great adaptive ability on the part of any creature living in it, and physiologically, the human species is one of the least adaptable species on this earth. Man's sole advantage, and the one that has raised humans so far above the animal kingdom, is the ability for cultural adaptation. But even this great advantage is double-edged. Though cultural adaptation to a new environment is possible, it is also extremely difficult. Where physiological adaptation takes place by necessity, in obedience to the power of natural forces to select only those who adapt, cultural adaptation depends on the willingness of the people involved to change their life-styles, values, and expectations in accord with their environment. And this, it appears, is one of the hardest things for human beings to do. Instead of adapting to the desert, they have tried to make the desert adapt to them, and throughout history they have failed. The desert has always defeated attempts at establishing large-scale human civilization, as though there were something inherently antisocial in it.

Men have conquered others many times in the Sinai and Negev, but they have never conquered the desert itself. The ruins of ancient civilizations that came into the desert in war and left it, again in war, are pathetic testimony to man's short-lived attempts to conquer the desert. The conquerors have long disappeared into the lost reaches of history, and only the desert remains. Who, then, was the conqueror, if not the desert itself?

Those who conquered this desert in the past—Nabataeans, Romans, Byzantines, Arabs, Turks, British, to count only the history of the last two thousand years—had no lasting influence on it. But the most recent conquerors, the Israelis, determined that they would change the course of history. In 1948, they became the first to venture into this desert not as an extension of empire, but as part of a deep historical sense of homecoming, a return to the place where their ancestors had roamed long before the empires of the world had come and gone. They brought with them a second order of conquering: aware that it was not enough to conquer the desert in war, they would now conquer it in peace. This was to become a proud ideology. But like all pride, it carried within it the seeds of downfall, for no matter how good the intention, one can only conquer by violence, and the act of conquering risks demeaning both conqueror and conquered.

The new state of Israel was to discover this the hard way, through experience. Meanwhile, as if in fulfillment of Nikos Kazantzakis's dictum in his essay on the Sinai that "We should always set the Impossible as our goal," the Israelis set about to do what seemed impossible. Using a unique blend of naïve idealism and pragmatic determination, they would conquer the desert by developing it, humanizing it, changing it completely into what they dreamed of as a place fit for human civilization.

The impassioned, white-haired prophet of Israel's drive into the desert was David Ben-Gurion, the country's founding statesman. A short, stocky man with the set features of absolute determination, he quickly grasped the political significance of the Negev: 60 percent of the country's territory, it was the bridge between East and West, Israel's opening to Africa and Asia through the Red Sea port of Eilat. Without it, Israel would be merely a tiny enclave on the eastern shore of the Mediterranean. But the bridge would have to be settled if it was to be used; it could not be allowed to remain desert. The basis of Ben-Gurion's thinking on the desert was thus a far-reaching strategy for building up Israel's economic and political independence. But there was also a visionary side to his determination. Coining the term "making the desert bloom," he saw it as a symbol for the rebirth of the Jewish people from the ashes and desolation of the Holocaust and exile. He exalted the pioneering spirit, "the moral treasure that springs from man's faith in his capacity to overcome obstacles . . . that would seem at first glance too formidable for the ordinary mortal." "The desert can be conquered by precisely such faith," he declared, since it stems from "man's burning spiritual need to transform the natural order, as well as the order of his own life, for the sake of the redeeming vision." Conquering the desert would nurture the qualities required for the redemption of his people.

Ben-Gurion therefore declared war on "this gloomy, uninviting, arid desert," issuing a call to arms for "an all-inclusive onslaught" on it. He hated the desert. Here was no idealist who loved the desert, but an ideologue who loved what the desert could become.

One of the apocryphal stories about "B.-G." that have multiplied since his death in 1973 relates to the time when he had retired to Kibbutz Sde Boker in the central Negev. A constant stream of visitors came to see him at work on the kibbutz, and he would ask each one what he or she had seen in the desert. They would tell him of wadis and mountains, of kibbutzim and development towns. But he would merely frown and reply crustily: "You didn't see the main thing; you didn't see what *isn't* in the desert." The desert was only the blank canvas on which Ben-Gurion and those inspired by his ideology would work. It was both a reproach and a challenge.

The challenge was taken up with a vengeance. Within twenty years, Israel had converted the semiarid areas between Tel Aviv and Beersheba, fifty miles to the south, into fertile farming land. Where once the Negev began just south of Tel Aviv, it now started at Beersheba, just within the ten-inch rainfall line generally accepted as the border of a desert area.

With the semiarid land reclaimed, Israeli farmers and scientists now began the onslaught on the desert itself. They would do in the desert what they had done on its northern border—farm it, settle it, and change it into civilized territory.

But the desert remains true to itself despite modern man and his aspirations. Caesar-like, man comes and sees not the validity of the desert, but the possibilities for conquering it. As technology develops, so too do the means by which man can impose his culture upon even the most hostile environment, forcing it to his will. Or so he imagines.

Israel's ideology of conquering the desert was intricately bound up with its fight for physical survival as a state. But this fight has created a tragic double bind. After more than thirty years, Israel still cannot take its existence for granted; it is still threatened from without. And a country so deeply involved for so long in the basic strategies of survival has had little care for the quality of that survival. That, it was thought, was something that would come of itself. But it never does. And nowhere is this more poignantly true than in the desert, for part of the desert's power is its uncompromisingly harsh revelation of man's treatment of it.

There are five towns in the Negev apart from Beersheba, each of them standing gaunt and repellent against the desert. Walled in by apartment blocks, each block within spitting distance of the next, they seem like fortresses turned in on themselves in a futile attempt to resist the force of the desert outside. They are called "development towns." Built with no regard for the environment in which they are placed, they look from afar as if some tired planner in a fit of perversity had placed a handful of cubes here and there on the landscape just to prove that it was possible. Then the contractors had come to pour their concrete walls, trying to barricade the desert out of their consciousness lest their souls shrivel in fear of these immense vistas.

Three of these towns in particular—Yeruham, Dimona, and Mitzpe Ramon—epitomize the degradation of both man and desert, the conqueror and the conquered. Yeruham, for example, rises starkly from a hill in the central Negev, on a side road off a side road. Below the town, a long row of storehouses fronts the road, and on them is scrawled in large black letters: YERUHAM, TOWN WITHOUT PITY. The slogan is from Yeruham's battle with the authorities some years ago to get a doctor for the town's six thousand residents. But it remains as a haunting motto for the town itself. The place has a pitiless air to it, the soulless empty feeling of the human desert. Between the sterile apartment blocks, sand blows listlessly over the asphalt streets; within their concrete restraints the vitality of the people living in them is drained to the point where many residents call for abolishing the town altogether. Its structure and design are a painful realization of its planners' hate for the desert. The writing on the wall is echoed in the hearts of those forced into this enclave, for the hate with which the town was built can only engender further hate in those who must live there.

Most of the people in the development towns did not choose the desert. For the most part, they are North African immigrants and their children who were dispatched straight to the Negev the moment they came off the boats in the 1950s, fodder for the dream of developing the desert. But while the mere presence of people can indeed conquer a desert, it is a short-lived victory. The desert demands its own. And if those living there are not willing to adapt themselves to it, then the desert claims a terrible revenge. The dream becomes a nightmare—a dream, like Yeruham and like the new industrial villages for the Beduin, without pity and without humanity: a human desert. This is the desert of fear, and the desert to be feared.

The imperative of the desert and its revenge on human misuse of it can be even harsher than this, forcing man to create his own deserts—not only the mindless automatism that we think of as the desert of the mind, but also the physical desert, the barren rock covered only with dust. The ideological approach of conquering the desert risks creating human deserts. But the traditional approach by which small nomadic populations have existed in the desert and on its borders for hundreds if not thousands of years is now creating physical deserts in which man is being conquered by famine and drought.

The true deserts of the world remain so regardless of man, but the semiarid steppelands bordering deserts are extremely labile. If wisely cultivated, they can be fertile; but if the demands on such areas are too many and the techniques are out of tune with its ecology, they become barren. This is the phenomenon of "the creeping desert," of what the United Nations has called "desertification."

Desertification first began to alarm the world after the drought in North Africa's Sahel zone in the early seventies. Three consecutive years of lower-than-average rainfall sufficed to cause yet-untold misery and death all along this belt of land bordering the southern Sahara. What was steppeland at the beginning of the drought was desert by the end of it. But it was not the climate that was to blame. Over the last eight thousand years, the climate of these regions has remained the same, its main characteristic being that it is highly unpredictable, with one year's rainfall maybe just a third or a quarter of that of the previous year. A rapid increase of population without a corresponding change in methods and life-style under such conditions could only lead to disaster. The horrible truth is that the people who starved and died in the Sahel zone did so because they were no longer living in tune with the land and their demands on it, because they had not developed a true desert agriculture that would feed their numbers by raising the level of the desert ecosystem. Instead, they destroyed it.

Desertification is an entirely manmade phenomenon, and its prime cause is overuse of the land. In most desertification zones, pastoralism is the main mode of income. But as the human population has increased in the last decades, so too has the population of flocks. As their goats, sheep, and cattle graze more and more of the sparse steppe vegetation, pastoralists must let their flocks wander wider in search of fodder, and in dry years wider still. Overgrazing denudes the land of its native vegetation, leaving nothing to protect the thin soil of the steppe against erosion by winds and flash floods. The vegetation has no chance to regenerate and the whole ecosystem begins to downgrade.

Even where attempts have been made to abandon pastoralism for irrigated farming, disaster has often resulted due to bad irrigation and cultivation methods. Overirrigation, for instance, leads to waterlogged soil in which the salinity level rises dangerously, creating a salt desert. This is what happened to the great irrigation cultures of the Tigris-Euphrates valley thousands of years ago. Urban demand for fuel has also speeded up the desertification cycle. Firewood is the main fuel in many developing countries, and both cities and pastoralists must cast farther and farther afield for wood as they denude the areas around them of woodland and shrub, laying the soil bare to erosion. Since the human population growth is more rapid by now than the regrowth of woody material in such areas, natural growths of forest and steppelands have been depleted, and in some areas eradicated. Badly planned modernization aids desertification in countless ways, among them the advent of the cash economy, which has made agriculture more profitable than pastoral farming. Good grazing lands have been taken over for cultivation, indigenous vegetation removed to clear plots, and the tractor brought in to plow them. Where the traditional hand-plow merely turned the soil, the tractor now loosens it, making it more liable to erode. As more land is cultivated, the pastoralists have been squeezed into increasingly marginal areas, setting off another round of desertification by overgrazing ever-poorer pastures. Desertification thus becomes a continuing spiral, a slow but unrelenting "scorched-earth" process.

But there does exist a third option, a viable alternative to the imposition of ideology and to the surrender of traditionalism. In 1953, when Israel was planning the first of its desert development towns, a call for a radically different relationship to the environment came from Aldo Leopold, one of the American fathers of conservation. His *A Sand County Almanac* had been printed some years before, and now he published a short but persuasive essay advocating what he called "the land ethic." This ethic, he wrote, "changes the role of *Homo sapiens* from conqueror of the land to plain member and citizen of it. It implies respect for his fellow members, and also respect for the community as such. . . . We can be ethical only in relation to something we can see, feel, understand, love, or otherwise have faith in." To see, feel, understand, love, or have faith in the desert, modern man would have to come to it in harmony, not discord, with the intention of living *with* the desert instead of against it. He would have to break the stranglehold of fear of the desert and accept it in all its grandeur and expanse and all its harshness.

An ethical relationship to the desert is a difficult proposition, but an essential one—no mere mystical luxury, but a vital condition for human survival in it. In the short term, an ideology can conquer the desert, but in the long term the desert produces bitter fruits of victory as though in contemptuous derision of human attempts to bring it to heel, to ignore its imperative, and to wrest from it what it is unwilling to give. The soft approach of the ethic may be able to persuade the desert to give sweet fruit. Instead of wresting from the desert it coaxes; instead of imposing human technology and culture, it attempts to work with the desert in acknowledgment of the fact that while it may not be conquered, its ecological level may be gradually raised to a level where human beings, too, may become part of a healthily functioning desert ecosystem.

The ethical approach deals in terms not of control, but of harmony. It relates neither to man nor to the environment exclusively, but to the interrelationship between them, in acknowledgment of the fact that man is as dependent on his environment for growth and stability as it is on him. It accepts the limitations imposed by the environment and respects them because it aims not at conquering, nor at simple physical survival, but at harmonious existence.

The guidelines for putting such an ethic into practice have been established by the economist E. F. Schumacher in *Small Is Beautiful*, a call for a radical reorganization of science and technology "towards the organic, the gentle, the non-violent, the elegant and the beautiful." Ironically, while it has completely ignored these guidelines in its urbanization of the desert, Israel has adopted just such an approach in its latest work in desert agriculture. As a tiny country with sparse natural and financial resources, Israel's good fortune is that it has no option but to think small. Years of pouring fresh water from the north into the Negev kibbutzim have made it clear that unless they are heavily subsidized, the kibbutzim cannot exist on such expensive water. To be economically viable, to be self-sufficient even, alternate water sources—desert sources—have to be adopted.

One possible alternative is rainfall. Ancient systems of harnessing the sparse desert rainfall fit the desert ethic superbly. They have been reconstructed and improved upon to create an elegant farming system that fits perfectly into the flow of natural desert phenomena. But no kibbutz is willing to base its livelihood on so unpredictable a thing as rainfall. A more promising if less elegant alternative is one that some kibbutzim have already adopted—using the brackish water found beneath the desert in shallow aquifers or in deep fossil "oceans." Rain above and oceans below—both are desert resources previously ignored or hitherto unknown in the modern search for a desert livelihood. The use of rainfall arose out of a desert ethic, while the impetus to develop brackish water resources was ideological; but both, the former by choice and the latter by necessity, are "small is beautiful" approaches to desert agriculture.

10 · Rain

Agriculture in the desert seems an impossible paradox. Most agriculture depends on direct rainfall, and the two to four inches of rain that fall in the central Negev each year are far below the minimum for such agriculture. It would seem that without artificial irrigation, there can be no such thing as desert agriculture. But that conclusion is merely the result of our own limitations of vision. The problem is not one of rainfall, but of knowledge: what we know prevents us from seeing what is there to be seen. Our very sophistication in dealing with data on paper prevents us from seeing the reality behind the data.

The only way to understand the potential of the desert rainfall is to live in the desert. It may rain four or five times a year, or only once, or even not at all. There is never any telling where it will rain or when. You simply have to be there, and wait. Even then, the waiting can be very frustrating. The sky may be completely clouded over, colored a deep gray, sometimes almost cobalt blue, and yet no rain may fall. It may be a beautifully sunny day where you are, and yet at day's end companions will come back from a trip "just the other side of those hills," drenched from a downpour. But eventually, if you have patience, it will happen. The sky darkens completely as a huge black cloud hovers over the area, and suddenly water starts falling. Sharp heavy drops sting your skin and leave their imprints on the desert soil around you. Rocks glisten with abrupt moisture. And if the cloud is large and enough rain falls, you realize that the water is not being absorbed by the desert. An extraordinary thing happens. The water begins to rush down off the mountains and hillsides, sweeping down gullies and creeks to cascade through the wadis in the sudden sharp torrents that we call flash floods, carrying with it rocks, stones, and debris from the desert surface. Suddenly there is water everywhere. Brownish swirling torrents fill the wadi beds, curtains of water cover the rocks, and even waterfalls suddenly roar in those steep canyons where thousands of years of such sudden streams have met at a low point to cut through the rock and plunge free into the wadi below. The sky may start to clear, the sun may even emerge again, yet the water still runs off the hills and rocks, streaming through the wadis eastward toward the Great Rift Valley or westward toward the Mediterranean, to be absorbed finally in gravel or sand. There are rivers in the wadi beds for days after such a downpour, though the water moves sluggishly by then. And even a week later, there are still large puddles left in the bends of the wadis, and pools in dips within the rocks, to which the desert wildlife comes to drink in unaccustomed ease. Only half an inch of rain may have fallen, yet the remains of that rain are still visible a week later. This is the ancient secret of desert agriculture.

In much of the Sinai and Negev the topsoil is loess, a loamy silt deposit of clay and dust, which sits a foot to six feet thick atop the bedrock on the plains and on the slopes of the wadis. The loess absorbs relatively little water during rain: it forms a thin impermeable crust when the first raindrops hit it, so that the rain that follows runs off the soil much as it runs off rock. Obviously one can plant nothing on rock, but one could plant on the loess soil if there were only a way to make it absorb the rainwater. Ancient desert peoples found this way. Instead of standing by while the water rushed down off the rocks and over the loess to the wadi beds, they trapped it. They dug channels over the hillsides to act as conduits, guiding the "runoff" water down to the loess deposits where they wanted it. There, they built stone and earthen dams and retaining

walls in order to hold the water on top of the loess. When a
foot of rainwater had collected on such a walled-off plot, the
very weight of it would allow it to penetrate the hitherto-
impermeable loess barrier and enter the soil. This could take a
week or more, but it was a worthwhile wait. Soil that had
been practically rock-hard could now be plowed and planted
with unusual success. Once thoroughly dampened, loess is
particularly fertile, because it retains water longer than most
soils—long enough to bring up a good crop of barley or wheat
with no additional rainfall.

To prevent erosion by flash floods in particularly heavy
downpours, the ancient farmers planned their farms in
terraces and built in an intricate stabilizing system to spread
the water by means of spillways, dividing boxes, and stone
sluices. The exact calculations determining the angles of the
miles of conduits leading down from the hills and the size of
the terraces and catchment basins on the plains and the wadi
slopes were quite sophisticated. But it takes only elementary
arithmetic to calculate the amount of water accumulated by
this method. Runoff water may be as much as half the total
rainfall, the rest being absorbed into the rock, caught in pools,
or evaporated. At a minimum, the runoff is one-quarter of the
rainfall. Thus if there were four inches of rainfall in one year,
at least one inch would be runoff water. The total catchment
area for each cultivated plot was generally about thirty times
the size of the plot, so that if one acre was cultivated, the
conduits and channels feeding it with water would cover
about thirty acres of hillside. Thus any cultivated plot would
receive four inches of rainfall, plus the one inch of runoff
water from an area thirty times its size—totaling thirty-four
inches of rain, the equivalent of the annual rainfall in southern
England. By using the surplus of water after a desert
downpour, the ancients converted four inches of rain into
thirty-four!

The most innovative of these ancient desert farmers were
the Nabataeans, a people who would be the stuff of myth and

legend were the greater story of Christ not unfolding in the Judean Desert when they were at the peak of their power in the Sinai and the Negev. In the second century B.C., this nomadic tribe swept westward and northward out of Arabia to establish a vast desert kingdom—an arc from Damascus down through Transjordan and the whole of Arabia through the Negev to the Sinai and the Mediterranean coast. Within a hundred years, they had established full control of the trade routes of the desert, gaining an absolute monopoly on all goods traveling east or west. Their caravans carried myrrh and frankincense from Arabia, spices and tea from India, silks and perfumes from China to satisfy the jaded appetites of first the Greek and then the Roman empires in the west. With amazing speed, they learned to use seafaring ships as cleverly as they used the ships of the desert. These once-primitive nomads became a sophisticated trading people using both military might and agricultural inventiveness to secure their rule over this great desert bridge between the riches of the kingdoms of the east and the greed of those of the west. At the peak of Nabataean power, their caravan routes crisscrossed the deserts of the Middle East in all directions—westward to the Mediterranean, north to Damascus, and south and east to the seaports of Gerrha on the Persian Gulf, Leuce Come on the Red Sea, and Aden. There was even a special "black route" used to carry bitumen from the Dead Sea to Egypt for embalming ceremonies.

Their center was the Great High Place of Zibb Atuf at Petra, the stunning temple city carved out of the red sandstone mountains of Moab, a focal point in the desert triangle of Arabia, the Negev and the Sinai. Here, they held their cultic feasts and fertility rites, and made blood sacrifices to a stunning pantheon of gods for a desert people—to Baal Haddad, the god of rain who held a thunderbolt in his hand and who had given them the wisdom to use the waters of the heavens; to Atargatis, half woman, half fish, the mermaid goddess of fertility who was consort to Haddad; and to the dolphins that were Atargatis's playmates, the dolphins that were their guides through the desert, that played around the prows of their ships on the high seas, and that would guide them once again on the longest voyage of all, after death. Their very gods were tribute to the Nabataeans' sophistication. In the vast trackless mystery of the desert they established trade routes and harnessed the desert rainfall in cisterns and farms. Where peoples before them had thirsted for water in the desert, the Nabataeans grew vines and quenched their thirst on wine.

The Nabataean capital of the Negev was Avdat, a tough two-day journey from Petra as the caravans descended the Moab Mountains into the blast of stifling heat of the Great Rift Valley, south of the Dead Sea, where the air hangs still and silent and the wells are brackish. Set on a flat-topped hill in the central Negev, the ruins of Avdat still glow in the setting sun like a delicate jewel set so gracefully into the mountaintop that it seems as though the rock itself had risen up to trace golden arches and pillars against the deepening blue of the sky. It must have taken supreme pride and confidence to build such a city, and engineers and hydrologists of great sophistication to plan the runoff farms and design the cisterns in the hillsides so that the desert rainfall would assure the ten thousand people who once lived there of water enough for both their own needs and those of the passing caravans. Though the Nabataeans did not invent the runoff system, they developed it to the point where it could sustain an empire. They reconstructed the poor farms built by the Israelites of Solomon and David a thousand years before and improved on them. Where the Israelites had merely built dams to hold the runoff water, the Nabataeans built hundreds of miles of terraces and channels throughout the desert, adding diversion conduits and aqueducts to ensure that the maximum of runoff water was used. Within the rock itself, they built covered cisterns instead of open ones, and even built their houses with sloping roofs so that each household could collect its own private runoff cistern of drinking water. Their garrisons became settled desert centers guarding the great network of trade routes on which depended the wealth and might of the Nabataean Empire.

The Nabataean form of Aramaic spread through the deserts of the Middle East, replacing other forms to become the major desert tongue and script. The thunderbolt, the mermaid, and the dolphin became the gods of the desert, and the Nabataeans became justifiably proud of their desert prowess and empire and of the independence that their knowledge of desert rainfall and its uses accorded them. While the Judeans suffered under Roman rule to the north, the Nabataeans capitalized on Roman greed for goods from the east. Yet they cannot have been unaware of the changing political climate of the Middle East, of the increasingly harsh rule of the Romans over the peoples to the north and the disintegration of what was by now the puppet Judean kingdom.

The last great Nabataean king, Aretas IV, ascended his throne just three years before Jesus was born, and despite himself was caught up in the epic of Christ. To consolidate his power in the Judean Desert, he married his favorite daughter to the Judean king Herod Antipas, one of the few surviving sons of the paranoid Herod the Great. But Herod abandoned his Nabataean wife for the lures of his sister-in-law Heroditas. When John the Baptist denounced the pair for transgressing Jewish laws of incest, Heroditas developed a vituperous hate for him, a hate that claimed the Baptist's life when Herod, entranced by the dancing of Heroditas's daughter, offered the girl anything she wanted—and the mother told the girl to claim the head of John the Baptist on a platter.

When his daughter fled back to Nabataea to escape the poison of Heroditas, Aretas must have considered the dangers of the dissolution of the Judean Kingdom and of the expanding iron grip of the Roman Empire. But his pride in his own kingdom may have blinded him to the force of history. If he had sat in the hilltop city of Avdat that year, A.D. 32, he could have looked down through the archways and pillars and seen the orchards of olives and dates, figs and almonds, pomegranates and peaches ripening in the plains and valleys below. Fields of wheat and barley lay strewn in the wadis like soft-woven sheep-wool rugs, and beyond them stretched the carefully tended vineyards, the vines gently bent over to shade the grapes swelling and ripening on their underside. Fingering his shiny tight ringlets and smoothing his oiled moustache, Aretas might have reflected that the thunderbolt, the mermaid, and the dolphins had served him well and might have offered a libation to them, watching the stone dolphins leap about the head of Atargatis in the golden light of sunset. But despite the idyllic scene below him, he may also have longed for the sense of invincibility of his rock temple-fortress of Petra. There, in the wilds of the desert mountains, he could have felt that his kingdom was everlasting. Here in Avdat, just one hundred miles south of Jerusalem, he must have had some premonition that both pride and empires must fall.

Aretas lived to hear of Christ's death the following year, but died himself four years later. It took only seventy years more for the dolphins to abandon their desert masters and return to their native seas. A new empire had gained power in the desert.

The Romans could not tolerate the Nabataean monopoly on trade from the east, but neither could they penetrate the desert. Instead, they went around. They opened a northern trade route overland, eastward from Palmyra, and another southern route down the Nile from Alexandria and thence to the western coast of the Red Sea, thus bypassing the area of Nabataean hegemony. The desert caravan highways declined in importance, and the power base and riches of the Nabataeans were gradually eroded. In A.D. 106, the Romans occupied the Nabataean Empire without resistance, and annexed it to the Roman Empire as Arabia Petraea. Since they did not need the desert itself, they merely kept it subdued. The Nabataeans slowly dispersed—perhaps back into Arabia again, though no one knows for sure. Their cities reverted to mere garrison posts for the Romans, and their farms were all but neglected.

It was not until the fourth century that the events of Aretas's time came full circle in the desert. The followers of John the Baptist and Jesus of Galilee had become Christians, and Christianity had spread and its influence increased until Constantine declared it the official religion of the Byzantine Empire. By that time, the northern trade route to the Far East through Palmyra was blocked by continuous wars with the Persians, and the desert route again came into its own. The Byzantines restored the Nabataean cities, effacing the Nabataean gods where they could and building churches and altars of their own. The desert became a monastic center, and pilgrims began to arrive in search of the famed hermits who lived there, demanding food, water, and shelter. The Byzantines were quick to grasp the principles of desert agriculture, and they rebuilt and improved on the Nabataean farms, bringing the art of intensive desert cultivation and rainfall storage to a peak of sophistication. But their kingdom too, as Aretas could have told them, was destined to end, as all empires must.

By the beginning of the seventh century, Byzantium could no longer protect its southernmost provinces. The Persians overran Antioch and then Jerusalem and even reached Avdat until the Byzantines managed to fight them back again . . . only to encounter a new threat from the south—the rising banner of Islam. The Arabs swept north and west out of Arabia, bringing with them the word and the sword of the Prophet Muhammad. They took Damascus, then Jerusalem, then the Negev and finally the Sinai and Egypt. But they were aiming for the cities, not for the desert, and though they drove the Byzantine rulers out of the Sinai and Negev, they replaced them with none of their own. The nomads of the desert began to take what they could, raiding the settled population, destroying farms and cities, and then moving on. Within a century, the desert that had supported a hundred thousand people no longer had any settled population. Flash floods that had once watered farms now eroded the abandoned terraces. A few scraggy goats grazed where once barley had flowered in the wadis. Where pomegranates had ripened, now only thornbushes grew. The desert, it seemed, had returned to its own. There were no longer men in sufficient numbers to make it either flourish or die. It became again the desert that had existed long before the Israelites or the Nabataeans or the Byzantines, and for the next twelve hundred years, only a few Beduin tribes eked out a living where once tens of thousands had lived in prosperity—until, in the early twentieth century, the descendants of the Israelites began to return to Palestine, bringing with them a new determination to tame the desert in the south.

One of these future Israelis, however, had no such intention. He loved the desert far too much to want to tame it. Walter Schwarz arrived in Palestine in 1933, at age twenty-eight, and within a year took a new name, a Hebrew one. Since his mother's maiden name was Loewenstein, his Hebrew name would be Evenari, "Stone Lion." He Hebraized his first name too, and became Michael Evenari. Born in France, he had spent the whole of his academic career in Europe, first in Frankfurt, then in Prague, and finally as a lecturer in botany at Darmstadt University, Germany. In 1933, Darmstadt expelled him because he was a Jew. (Ironically, the same university was to award him an honorary doctorate in 1977.) The future Evenari was ready to leave in any case, for he had been offered a job researching desert plants in Palestine. He was already a Zionist, and Hitler's policies merely triggered his decision to take up the job offer. But today he admits that it was neither Zionism nor Hitler that brought him there. It was the desert. And it was his love for and fascination with the desert that would eventually prompt him to a full-scale reconstruction of the ancient Nabataean system of runoff farming.

Today, though in his mid-seventies, Evenari is still young

and full of zest, a tall round-faced man with an infectious smile, extraordinarily smooth skin, and high cheekbones, which give him a slightly Oriental appearance. In the desert, he wears shorts and a big floppy hat over his wispy-haired head; in Jerusalem, where he is professor of botany at the Hebrew University, he wears a three-piece suit resplendent with gold watch chain, and smiles as he comments on his city camouflage. But the three-piece suit is hardly worn, for it has always been hard to keep the man out of the desert. He was in the Judean Desert the day after he got off the boat from Europe in 1933, and in the next few years he took long swings throughout the deserts of the Middle East. Today such trips can be done in weeks, but then they took months. Jeeps had not yet been invented, for World War II was still to come, and the traveler had to rely on the Model-T Ford to take him from camel to camel.

The critical year was 1936, when Evenari visited Petra in Transjordan and was deeply impressed by this first glimpse of Nabataean culture. Arching back through the Negev to Jerusalem, he began to see the remains of Nabataean agriculture in practically every wadi, on nearly every hillside—the conduits and dams, terraces and channels, all in ruins yet discernible to the practiced eye. But the Negev was still too dangerous a place in those years for a scientist to wander unhindered. Evenari and his colleagues had to wait until 1949, after Israel's War of Independence, to explore the Negev as they wanted. By then another member had joined the small company—Evenari's blond wife Liesel, who accompanied him on all his travels from 1948 on. Now they no longer needed special permits to venture into the desert. The fledgling Israeli army could provide them with a modicum of security, though their jeeps still had to travel convoy-style, with one-fifth of the company on guard at any one time. There were no roads as yet, but jeep tracks crisscrossed the desert as the army carved out patrol routes, sometimes reopening the ancient caravan routes. The more Evenari saw, the greater was his fascination with the fact that there had evidently once been a flourishing civilization in the desert. But how it worked remained a puzzle, a challenge to the ingenuity of the modern scientist.

That challenge came to a peak one hot day in August 1956. "We were near the ancient town of Shivta," Evenari wrote many years later in *The Negev: Challenge of a Desert*. "As usual we had settled down for a short siesta in the shade of blankets strung between two jeeps and were digesting the famous Liesel Evenari desert salad made of desert plants and cultivated vegetables. The desert heat and flies did not allow us to doze off, so we drowsily discussed farfetched theories. It was at this point that one of us threw out the idea: 'Would it be feasible to reconstruct an ancient farming system and make it work? The archaeologist only reconstructs towns; let's reconstruct a farm.' Now we all sat up, wide awake, startled and fascinated by the idea. We argued vigorously, some for, some against the proposal. . . ."

The more they discussed the project, the more exciting it became. At first, they thought merely to prove or disprove existing theories about the principles of ancient runoff farming. Then they saw that if they planned the reconstruction carefully, they could gather invaluable information about the desert climate, rainfall, and runoff. Finally, they realized that here was a chance to see to what extent runoff farming could be used in the twentieth century—could it be agriculturally viable?

To find out, the Evenaris "went Nabataean." In the summer of 1959, they and their colleagues began to reconstruct one of the largest farms in the Avdat area, right below the ruins of the hilltop city. In early December, after the first rain, they planted barley; to their delight, it grew! The next year, the Evenaris built a small dual-purpose home and laboratory on a hill overlooking both the farm and the ruined city. When they moved into the house, "we changed from visitors to citizens of the desert," says Evenari. "We became heirs to an old civilization and way of life that had disappeared many centuries ago."

Evenari had finally found the fulfillment of his love for the desert. "I had a romantic idea about the desert long before I saw it," he reminisces today, leaning on the wooden refectory table in the small stone house and slowly puffing a ragged cigar. "It all came from books, of course, especially Doughty's *Travels in Arabia Deserta*. That was romantic not in the sentimental meaning of the word, but in the way that it opened up one's soul and one's senses. Those descriptions of the desert nights, for example," he says, spreading his arms expansively, "those nights of sitting around the fire with the darkness of the desert all about, telling stories and sipping cup after cup of coffee. Wonderful! And yes, even the descriptions of the harshness of the desert summer are wonderful. After all, isn't that the very thing that's attractive for a scientist? It means that the desert is a natural laboratory, with the one limiting factor, water, well isolated. The desert is the perfect place for experiments on plants under water stress. How could I resist that as a botanist?

"But of course I mean romantic in a far more personal sense, too. I still remember the excitement of reading about Doughty's discovery of ancient inscriptions in the desert, the traces of ancient cultures. For me this is highly romantic, since it means that one can trace oneself back in the desert through a very long time. Don't forget, romanticism for me is part and parcel of this very Jewish trait of being closely tied to the past, of having a far deeper sense of history than most peoples. And a sense of history means for me an attachment to that history and a deep meaning in it." Now Evenari had found for himself in Avdat the romanticism he had sensed in Doughty's adventures.

Today, the Avdat farm covers eight acres planted with almond, pistachio, and peach trees. Another reconstructed runoff farm in Wadi Mashash, between Avdat and Beersheba, produces huge round olives, like tiny crab apples, and also like them, bittersweet. A third farm near Shivta, west of Avdat, has had to be abandoned for lack of funds, though the almond trees still blossom there in midwinter. In the intervening years, Evenari has worked out a detailed system of runoff farming, concentrating on perennial crops—mainly nut and fruit trees—in the plots that get the first of the runoff water, and field crops only in lower plots, which can be plowed if there is sufficient rain and left fallow if there is not. From 1960 on, he and his wife spent at least half of each year living in Avdat, whether six consecutive months, three months here and three there, or two weeks out of each month. But in 1977 Evenari had his first meeting with mortality in the form of a heart attack, and since then has been under doctor's orders to spend less time in the south and to take things easy, orders that do not come easy to a man with so much to do. He has satisfied his original curiosity and not only proved that the runoff system can work but also improved on it, and the results of his work can now be seen in places as far apart as Afghanistan and Australia. But he is far from finished with his research. Since the heart attack, he has been concentrating on collecting all his research data on desert plants and ecology for publication and on expanding the runoff system in an attempt to prove that it can be economically viable. His choice for this project was the pistachio tree, and in 1977, he planted a five-acre plantation of pistachios watered solely by rainfall runoff.

But it is still the desert itself that interests Evenari, rather than specifically agriculture. For many Israelis, he is the epitome of the Zionist ideology of "making the desert bloom," yet he himself detests that phrase. "I did what I did out of curiosity," he explains. "What better reason could there be? If you take away curiosity, there's very little left. We were scientists who wanted to see if our theory was correct, and the best way to do that was in the field. All the agricultural consequences were secondary. True, we're now working on proving that larger-scale runoff farming can be economically viable. But you know, all people have split personalities, and I suspect that mine is more deeply split than most. It's bad to say this as an Israeli, I know, and I'm rather ashamed of saying it, but I was never particularly interested in something economically viable as far as Israel is concerned, only for developing countries. For Israel I think it's counterproductive, because of the danger of overmechanization and the consequent destruction of the desert. But for developing countries, this could be vitally important."

As he talks, the air conditioning whispers. He apologizes for it: "It was only put in after the heart attack, otherwise we'd never have had it." Liesel sits in on our conversations, keeping a sharp eye lest her husband get overexcited, always conscious of the doctor's orders. She is still beautiful in her late sixties, with a splendid long mane of blond-gray hair, which she usually wears braided in the French fashion of the thirties. She has been his companion throughout his work, and though he would probably have done the same without her, one feels that he would not have enjoyed it nearly as much. The volunteer staff on the Avdat farm call her "the queen," and she has a certain regal air about her. What she says, goes, and when the conversation gets heated, as it tends to do because Evenari is passionate about his love for the desert and the dangers of overdevelopment, she changes the direction of the talk. Evenari raises his hands helplessly, looks at her fondly, and thumps on the table saying, "Yes, what next?"

He sums up his feeling about developing the desert in one anecdote. "Some years ago, an exploratory oil rig was drilling near Avdat. That put me in a very difficult situation. As a good Israeli, I should have prayed for an oil strike, for oil is one of the country's major problems. But we were both so happy when the rig failed and the engineers left. I understand the necessity for industrial development and the rationale behind putting chemical industries in the desert, but I'm extremely unhappy about it. Rationally I understand it; personally I hate it. It's like the joke about the difference between a madman and a neurotic: the madman says that two times two is five; the neurotic says that two times two is four, but he hates it. Dad 2 + 2 = 22, too!

"This ideology of conquering the desert, however, will never work. The desert may conquer us, but we will never conquer it, and when we think we have done so the desert gets its own back, and we find the human desert asserting itself in the form of labor strife at the Dead Sea potash works or the spiritual and social poverty of the development towns in the desert." Such thinking makes Evenari very much of a loner in Israeli scientific circles, despite his father-figure reputation. He finds that he has more of a common language with the desert traveler-researchers such as the Frenchman Theodore Monod than with Israeli scientists caught up in the ideal of conquering the desert. "You are faced with something much greater and stronger than yourself in the desert," he says, "something that is beyond conquering. There is a very strong religious element to this feeling, and even though I am not religious in the conventional sense, I consider it no chance of historical fate that all three of the world's monotheistic religions are very strongly linked to this desert. Its beauty is completely exclusive; nothing distracts you from it. There is a unity in its desolation and harshness, a oneness that perhaps explains why the idea of one God arose out of this desert. Take the empty black stone reg areas of the Sinai, for example, where the flint desert 'pavement' stretches off into the horizon. If someone told my wife and me to go off and live in a tent there for the rest of our days we would do it, because that is the power of the place."

This oneness, this unity of the desert, has grasped Evenari's imagination and energies. His work in ecology stresses the wholeness of the desert system and the magic of it. "What we are doing here at the Avdat farm is ecofarming in the best sense of the word," he says, thumping on the table as Liesel looks on with concern. "It fits into the system. We haven't imposed ourselves on the desert; we've adapted ourselves, our ideas, and our methods to the desert and established a creative harmony with it." And with a beatific smile, he adds: "This is the whole beauty of runoff farming."

Evenari's energies are running lower now, but he is still supervising new projects. One of these is a "desert park" alongside the young pistachio plantation. The park is a large circle bordered by the retaining earth mounds typical of runoff farming. It was planted in 1977, and its wide variety of desert trees and shrubs are still no more than calf-high. Yet within ten years the annual rains flooding down from the hillsides nearby and along the conduits into the park will have created a circle of shade here. By then, the huge piece of stone in the middle of the park will be hidden by foliage. It is about seven feet long, four feet wide, and at its highest point over five feet tall, and it has been carved by sculptor Ezra Orion into the form of a lion. A stone lion, in tribute to the man who bears the name Evenari. And sometimes, as I've sat on the earthen mound of the retaining wall looking out over the park, the ruined terraces beyond it, and beyond them the hills and mountains of the Negev, I have imagined that when mortality does finally meet up with Michael Evenari, here, beneath this stone lion in the shade of a desert park, is where he should lie.

11 · Oceans

Two thousand years ago, the Nabataeans worshiped dolphins in the Sinai and the Negev, as though by carving these sea creatures in stone they could bring the fertility of the oceans into the arid wilderness. How did this ancient desert people choose dolphins as the playmates of their mermaid goddess Atargatis and as their guides into the afterlife? Could they have had any idea that there are oceans under the desert? Could they have trapped dolphins by carving them into the desert stone in homage to the water trapped two thousand feet below the barren surface?

Why? is the eternal question of archaeology. We find the artifacts of ancient peoples—what they created—but Why? remains a matter of speculation, for it relates not to the concrete achievements but to the psychology of a long-lost culture, to the experiences and visions, feelings and perceptions of a people. Why the Nabataeans chose dolphins as their guides in the desert is a mystery. We do know that the Nabataeans were seafarers, since they bridged the empires of east and west by bringing goods to and from the shores of the Middle East deserts. They may have brought the vision of dolphins back with them from these sea voyages: as the dolphins accompanied their ships through the water, so they would accompany their camels through the seas of sand and rock. But they must also have suspected that the desert too was once sea.

No one can wander long through the desert without encountering the signs of a petrified sea—the fossil remains of sea creatures lying among the rocks of the surface, what was once water turned into stone. There are sea urchins, for example, and rudistids, mollusks shaped like ice-cream cones. And the skewed symmetry of ammonites, the huge flat spiral fossils of the precursors of today's nautilus. Whereas now there are only nine species of nautilus left in the world's oceans, there were once two or three hundred, their shells an accretion of chamber onto chamber in an ever-increasing spiral until they were as much as two feet in diameter. And as if these fossils were not sufficient indication of the presence, at some time, of water, the Nabataeans must surely have wondered too at the number of snails and wood lice, mollusks and crustaceans still living in the desert.

But from noting such signs to saying that there are oceans of water under the desert is a large step indeed. Such an assertion has a legendary quality to it, an element of magic as strong as that of the stone dolphins. We shall never know whether the Nabataeans suspected the existence of such oceans. But we do know that these oceans exist under most of the world's deserts, their water trapped deep down beneath the surface in the vast aquifers formed by the sandstone layers of the earth's crust. Geologists call these aquifers "fossil waters." And within them there may even be fossils of the precursors of today's dolphins, water creatures turned into stone just as the ancient nautiloids became ammonites.

It all seems highly improbable to the layman, but not to a hydrogeologist, that very special species of geologist. Where the geologist sees the desert as a playground, a place where geological time and space lie open before him, unobscured by the fripperies of trees and topsoil, houses and agriculture, the hydrogeologist—the scientist who searches for water within the earth—would seem to face a poor proposition in the desert unless, like Moses, he can strike water from rock. But then, that is precisely his aim.

Arieh Issar, one of Israel's leading hydrogeologists, achieved this aim by proving the existence of a huge fossil aquifer stretching from the central Sinai northeast into the Negev and southwest to the Suez. He is an improbable Moses. Nothing in his appearance suggests that his home is the harsh rock of the desert. At fifty-two, he has more of the teddy bear than of rock about him, a comfortably rounded, soft-spoken man with tightly curled, peppery white hair, who smiles constantly as he talks, as though his whole body were in relaxation as his mind works.

His office in the tiny village of the Desert Research Institute in Sde Boker, in the center of the Negev, is a small concrete cube lined with maps and satellite photographs pinned to the walls. The air conditioning hums away the heat of the afternoon sun outside. Yet only a couple of hundred yards away is the majestic vista of the Zin Canyon, a deep-cut display of geological time in layer after layer of eroded rock that changes in color and depth as the sun moves through the day.

In this place, where less than four inches of rain fall each year, we talk of water. Or at least I do. Issar talks of "waters," the direct translation of the plural Hebrew noun for water, a plural that emphasizes the importance of water in a tongue that grew out of the desert. He measures his waters in "cubes," an abbreviation for "cubic meters" that gives a reassuring sense of solidity and presence to the billions of cubic meters of water under the desert.

The story of how Arieh Issar found this "ocean" under the Sinai is a paradigm of inductive science and a warning of what the scientist involved may have to face as the price of his thinking. Issar tells it softly, but with the relish of one who was finally proved right and with an undertone of stubbornness that explains his persistence. The story begins not in the Sinai, but in Iran, where Issar worked for four years in the early sixties as a United Nations consultant. "Iran gave me a sense of scale," he recalls, "the kind of scale that you don't get in a country as small as Israel. It was the scale on which waters can travel hundreds of miles underground, a scale that enabled me to think in large terms." On his return to Israel in 1965, Issar found that an experimental well drilled on the shore of the Dead Sea had struck a rich aquifer of water in a Nubian sandstone layer. The geologist in charge had concluded that the water came from the nearby Hebron Mountains, which tower above the Dead Sea at that point. But Issar's newfound sense of scale told him otherwise. "I knew there was a broad surface belt of Nubian sandstone across the central Sinai. It runs deep underground to crop up again here and there in the Negev and on the coast of the Gulf of Suez. And I also knew that rich aquifers had been found in Nubian sandstone layers under the Sahara. So I had a strong feeling that these waters came not from the Hebron Mountains but from the Sinai. I said so, and this geologist laughed at me. Just laughed at me. He said, 'I'm saying these waters traveled thirty miles from an area with twenty-five inches annual rainfall, and you're saying they came two hundred miles from an area with two inches rainfall? That's crazy!' And I replied, 'Well, but we're not talking about the present. . . .' "

Issar, in fact, was talking about the distant past. This was not the usual groundwater found in shallow aquifers, refilled each year by rainwater, but fossil water: not fossilized, but from the time of human fossils. It was water that fell as rain during the last Ice Age—some ten thousand to thirty thousand years ago—and that has been stored since then deep in the earth. As Issar talks about this water, I become highly aware of geological time. I realize that I have never thought of the age of water. Who would, indeed, except a hydrogeologist?

Two years passed until Issar could prove his theory. The Six-Day War and Israel's conquest of the Sinai provided the opportunity. Scarcely had the war ended than he was down in the Sinai collecting water samples for isotope analysis, one of the hydrogeologist's main tools of detection. The isotopes act rather like fingerprints of water, allowing the scientist to trace both its history and its flow. The results were unequivocal: the water found in the Nubian sandstone beneath the shore of the Dead Sea was the same as that in the Sinai. It all came from the same giant aquifer formed in what had once, geological ages ago, been the marshlands of the central Sinai.

Issar and his team published their findings just after Tahal, Israel's national water-planning authority, published its own report saying that there could be no large quantities of water in the Sinai, because there was little rainfall and high evaporation there. "We were ridiculed," says Issar, gesturing as he recalls the frustrations of those years. "We were called fantasists, folklorists, all the dirty names that scientists can throw at each other. It was a very difficult time. You see, when you're facing a tremendous idea, you ask, 'If it's so simple, why didn't people see it?' Because it's *simple*, very simple! And then you start thinking, 'Well, maybe there's some huge mistake that *I* don't see: maybe it's I that don't see the big barrier, not they.' And then you do more and more tests, and every time the tests prove that you're right. . . . Today, I know there is a *psychological* barrier, that people are afraid of big ideas. I'm not the first to think that these waters were there, but others before me never insisted on the vast potential of the Nubian sandstone, because if they had done the calculations they'd have come to the *billions* of cubes that are there in the Negev and the Sinai—and then they would have faced ridicule because people 'know' that there are no waters there."

So how was it that Issar was ready to face that ridicule? He smiles broadly at the question. "First," he said, "I like to fight with people, and there's a special kind of people with whom I enjoy fighting. I like to throw out ideas and get a response from people; the bigger the idea, the more it excites me. But there's something else far more important than that. For years, I flew and drove all over the desert, and the question was always, Can we live here? The day that we realized that there are billions of cubes here, it was like opening up a new land! So I said, 'I *must* be right; this is something worth fighting for. Even if I fail, it will be worthwhile fighting for this idea.' Because, you see, once I *did* fail, near Eilat, when an American geologist claimed he had found water in the granites there. I was the only one to back him, and the well failed. That was in 1959, and it was a spectacular failure, with more than five million dollars invested, a great deal then for this country. So it was inevitable that people would bring up that failure and say 'It's just another of Issar's crazy ideas, like Eilat.' "

No one is saying that anymore. Today, Issar's discovery is generally accepted even by those scientists who so viciously attacked his inductive mode of thinking. Not that Issar is unaware of the risks involved in such thinking. "You see, even in applied science it's a matter of, not intuition, but something else . . . data that you compute and then somewhere along the line you jump a few steps and come to a conclusion. It's dangerous; you always have to go and calculate the steps back. But you must make that leap into the dark. You see, if scientists become technologists, they'll degenerate," he says, using a favorite word. "They must be philosophers too." *and artists.*

Perhaps it was inevitable that Issar should have a strong philosophical bent. The son of Hasidim, Jewish mystics who came to Palestine as children from Russia and Lithuania at the turn of the century, he received a religious education throughout high school. By the time he was fifteen, he had realized that religion raised too many questions for him to accept it fully. But although today he is agnostic, the influence of Jewish thinking and ethics on his approach to science is clear. He sees Israel's desert science as part of the continual Jewish search for further development, of a relentless desire to change and improve the world in the search for a continually higher level of existence. One of his favorite topics in philosophy is the role of the perceiving mind. The usual historical coordinates of space and time, he argues, do not explain the development of human intelligence. To do that, one would have to add a third coordinate of the perceiving mind itself. In doing so, one would span the gap between the mechanistic and the animistic approaches. The former uses only the coordinates of space and time; the latter, only those of time and mind. But all three, he maintains, are necessary to understand the development of the mind itself.

The philosophy and history of science is Issar's hobby. But his driving force is ideology—the ideology of developing the desert, of turning it to man's needs and using the resources hidden deep within it to make it a place for human civilization. He and his generation in Israel were nurtured on this ideology, and he notes with great pride that he has managed to pass it on to his sons: one is studying biology at the Ben-Gurion University of the Negev in Beersheba, while the other is completing specialized studies in agriculture prior to settling in a commune in the Arava Desert, south of the Dead Sea. All three, father and sons, live and work in the tradition of conquering the desert.

This means that Arieh Issar and I have an ongoing conflict. It is played out quietly, in soft-spoken conversations in his home at Sde Boker, across the desk in his office a hundred yards away, or over the table in the communal dining hall built at the edge of the Zin Canyon, with its ageless view. It is the classical conflict between the conservationist and the developer, a conflict that I never expected to join before I went to live in the desert. I never dreamed that I would grow to love the desert with the passion that I do, nor that I would begin to see what was to me a proud national ideology as a threat to what I love. Perhaps the first sign of that conflict came one day as I was driving across the central Negev hills toward Sde Boker. As I came down off the hills toward the kibbutz, I saw the square green fields of alfalfa growing on the small plain below, irrigated by sprinklers. A customary sight, but that day it seemed that another part of me was seeing it. The fields were a masterpiece of human determination, of the impossible made real. Yet I felt a strange sense of discomfort, a discomfort that has increased since then and that now hits me full force each time I round that last bend in the mountain road and see those fields. No, I thought that day, that's wrong, that doesn't belong here. Green fields are for the north; they are too tame, too pretty for the desert. This is not desert agriculture; it's northern agriculture transplanted by technology into the desert.

One day, I faced Arieh Issar with this feeling. He took a deep breath and paused awhile, considering me. He knows a romantic when he sees one. And then softly, slowly, he answered. "I can understand your feeling. But you were not educated toward the idea of development, an idea we drank in with our mother's milk. To develop the land, to create another settlement, another kibbutz—this has always been part of my life.

"When I was a boy I used to walk in the Jerusalem hills, and there I could see all the destroyed terraces on the hillsides and the ruins of ancient towns. Now for some people these are very picturesque, but I feel just the sheer *insult* of creative work destroyed. All those terraces were worked once. People lived in those towns. And it was all destroyed, all left to ruin! Maybe you just have to get this kind of seeing into your system until you're provoked by waste. When you see a flash flood in a desert wadi, for instance, you probably see it as something wonderful, a spectacle. But for me it's a waste; that water could have brought life. Nature is for people to live, to get out of it what they can; it's not to be wasted. Frankly, I can't see the desert—or any area at all for that matter—left undeveloped. I see development as the struggle to get bread out of the land, and I think that through this, man develops all the time, achieving a higher cultural level. The minute you stop developing, degeneration sets in. Every human society, every living creature, has to progress all the time, because in nature no progress means degeneration. So I have the very deep feeling that in order to achieve a full cultural life we must be in continual struggle, aiming onward. Now we in Israel have had to fight for survival. I hope that fight will stop soon. But after peace, if we still want to exist and make progress, we will need a mountain to climb. And I see the desert—the desert in Israel and deserts all over the world—as a way for humanity to climb that mountain."

I was on the edge of my chair with argument bursting out of me. For someone who has developed a passionate love for the desert as it is—its wildness, its vast expanses, its solitude, its grandeur—such talk is like a cape swung at a bull. I hate to think of what will happen when civilization tries to prove itself in the desert. All I can see is the pity and sadness of that grand wildness tamed, those gaunt expanses greened over, progress in the form of towns and factories, pollution and the destruction of the fragile desert ecosystem. No more ibex or gazelles, jackals or hyenas, snakes or scorpions; no more desert.

Issar lit another pipe as I talked, and settled back in his chair, frowning slightly. "I'm not saying we'll do anything by force," he said. "You can't. You have to do it by wisdom. The desert presents a wonderful synthesis of technical, cultural, and mental challenge. You have to be strong to take it up since the climate is harsh; but you also have to be social. Yes, social. I'm against preserving the desert, against this whole conserva-tionist approach, because it's antisocial. People are starving in the world, and the desert is a vast resource for agriculture. But to use it we have to raise the level of the desert environment. It shouldn't be destroyed, but it should be developed."

Whether the desert can be developed without destroying its ecological balance and thus risking a dangerous boomerang effect is still an open question, however. Issar acknowledges the problem, but insists that the only way to deal with it is head-on. "We know one thing for certain," he says, "and that's that you can't rebuild the desert by remote control. If we want to raise the ecological balance, we have to live with it and understand it. You can't live apart from the desert if you want to work with it; you have to be part of it."

An old-fashioned spirit of pioneering—the willingness to struggle, and the delight in it—brought people like Arieh

Issar into Israel's desert and underpinned the development of a special desert agriculture based on the brackish water found beneath the desert. The new desert agriculture is based on two principles: first, finding alternative water sources—the work of Issar and other hydrogeologists—and second, developing means of using these sources. Conventional agriculture with brackish water is doomed to failure, since the water is too saline for most plants. The breakthrough was a combination of concept and technology: the concept that desert agriculture requires a completely different approach than that used in humid or even semiarid zones, and the technology of drip irrigation. Originally developed to save water, drip irrigation was found to be ideal for use of brackish water. The system is a series of underground pipes that feed small but continuous amounts of water directly to plant roots, without any spraying from above. The control of both the amount and placement of the water meant that water of a far higher salinity could be used, since the general salinity of the soil is kept at a minimum. Indeed it soon became clear that some crops actually flourish on the combination of drip irrigation and brackish water. The salt stress induced in them increases certain properties, so that cotton plants produce more flowers on brackish water, and sugar beet has a higher sugar content.

Kibbutz settlements in the southern part of the Arava Valley have now based much of their economy on brackish water. Here, in this stifling gouge in the earth's crust running southward from the Dead Sea to Eilat, there may be two inches of rainfall a year, or none. If humans are to exist here at all, alternative water sources are vital. At present, the kibbutzim are using shallow aquifers of brackish water. These are renewed annually by the meager rainfall of the area or by groundwater running down into the Arava from the mountains on either side, and they are sometimes as close to the surface as a hundred feet. Though this water is four times as saline as was thought the limit for agriculture just twenty years ago, the kibbutzniks are now growing tomatoes, eggplants, peppers, onions, melons, cucumbers, and even flowers on it, carefully timing their efforts to get out-of-season fruits and vegetables onto the European market.

The prospects for application of the brackish water in the deep fossil aquifers discovered by Arieh Issar are thus excellent, for the fossil aquifers are far less brackish than the shallow ones. Where the latter have a chlorides content of up to two thousand parts per million (compared to up to three hundred for sweet water and up to twenty-five thousand for seawater), the fossil aquifers have a chlorides content of five hundred to one thousand parts per million. By desert standards, this is sweet water. Its use is still problematic since water-pumping technology has yet to solve the problem of pumping from depths of two thousand to three thousand feet. But once this problem is solved, the "sweet" fossil aquifers can provide twice as much water as the shallow aquifers for hundreds of years, and better water at that. There remains one harsh fact, however: like oil, the fossil aquifers are a one-time resource. If used wisely, they may triple the amount of usable water in the desert for generations; if used carelessly, as in a recent and horrendously expensive Libyan experiment, they may empty rapidly or become too saline for use. However wisely they may be farmed, though, they will run out one day. Hopes are that desalination will be economically viable by then, but just as research on solar energy was sadly lacking until the oil crisis became acute, so too research on desalination is marking time, bogged down by the expense of the methods now in use, in addition to the cost of pumping desalinated seawater into the heart of the desert.

The modern systems of drip irrigation do not have the beauty and harmony of the ancient runoff farming system. They lack the elegant simplicity of concept and the sense of natural flow that comes from watching runoff water stream smoothly over the ancient farms rehabilitated by Michael Evenari. Perhaps they cannot possibly have this elegance, since they are designed to be economically viable—meaning profitable—while the runoff system was designed simply to provide for the needs of those actually living in the desert. But today there are so many people living in the world's deserts that the harmony of old can no longer apply. The population explosion in North Africa's Sahel zone, for example, and the drought and famine that it created in the early seventies, leading to desertification, stress the need for a new concept of harmony—a harmony that includes modern technology. The Israeli work with brackish water is a major step toward developing a new desert technology, but many of the scientists involved are aware that technology alone is not enough and that breaking the desertification spiral is a complicated social, political, and cultural process. The economist E. F. Schumacher emphasizes that development starts not with goods, but with people and their education, organization and discipline. The Israelis were quick to grasp this principle a generation before Schumacher, partly because they had no agricultural tradition from which to break and therefore saw the whole problem with fresh eyes.

From their vantage point today, Israeli scientists can point out many options for the Sahel zone. For example, livestock and crops native to arid zones could be introduced into the area. Instead of cattle, camels could be bred for milk, since they give more and better milk under arid conditions than cows and require far less water. Instead of wheat and other grains, such crops as the jojoba "oil bean" and cotton could be grown, both of which thrive on the brackish water in subsurface aquifers; instead of open-field farming, intensive closed-system techniques could be introduced; drip irrigation could be used to grow fruit and vegetables in the Sahel just as successfully as in the Arava.

The Israelis see such proposals not as solutions, but as part of a new and different approach to farming in arid and semiarid zones, an approach that both uses and harmonizes with the ecosystem, on the principle that if men are to live in the desert in the twentieth century, they must understand it.

"We have the scientific energy, the intellectual energy," comments Arieh Issar. "And by using it wisely, we won't be imposing ourselves on the desert. If we use what is in the desert with wisdom, we can achieve a creative harmony with it. And that way, we can renew the world."

Desertification is no natural disaster that man can only suffer. There are oceans of water beneath the desert, and though that water is brackish, there are sophisticated farming techniques that make the use of that water not only possible but profitable. Drought and starvation are not necessary evils of arid zones, for as Israel has proved, the desert can be farmed.

Israel chose to develop its desert as much for political as for economic reasons. But politics has now created a double irony. Israel's pullback of its armed forces from the Sinai as part of the 1979 peace treaty with Egypt will close a large part of the Negev to agricultural development, since the army needs huge tracts for training grounds. Israel's own use of its new desert technology will thus be severely limited. But its use for other countries will not. Israel's desert scientists are both aware and pleased that their work could eventually prove of far greater practical value to other countries than to their own, and particularly to those countries suffering from desertification in the semiarid lands on the borders of the Sahara. Yet these very countries, the ones that could most benefit from Israel's know-how, refuse to adopt it since they still count themselves among Israel's political enemies. The peace agreement with Egypt could be the first step toward breaking this barrier, toward dealing practically, economically, and wisely with the problem of desertification. The problem is less one of know-how than one of politics. "This way, we can renew the world," says Issar. If, that is, the world is willing to renew itself.

12 · Land

In both Hebrew and Arabic, Beersheba, the main town of the Negev, means "Well of Seven" or "Well of the Oath." It was here that Abraham, father to both Isaac and Ishmael, to the Israelite and the Arab peoples, made a covenant with Abimelech, giving him seven ewe lambs in return for recognition of the fact that the well he had dug here was his. For thousands of years, from the time of Abraham until less than fifty years ago, the well of Beersheba served desert nomads of both races. Today, Beersheba is part of the state of Israel, a sprawling city of a hundred thousand people whose chemical industries are rapidly polluting the groundwater that made it famous throughout the ancient Middle East.

One day, as I waited in a brightly lit Beersheba café to meet a Beduin lawyer, I overheard an Israeli woman at the table beside me talking in English to a young man, apparently a nephew from abroad. She told him something of the history of the area, and mentioned that there was a new industrial village for the Beduin just outside the city at Tel Sheva, very near the ancient city of Abraham's well.

"What's the status of the Beduin?" he asked.

"Oh, we give them everything," she replied. "We give them medical services and schools and welfare and family allowances and employment. They're very well off with us."

She could have said simply "They're Israeli citizens," adding perhaps that as such they receive all the services she mentioned as part of their rights as citizens. But she did not. Nor would most Israelis. Yet the forty thousand Beduin of

Israel, most of whom live in the northern Negev, are indeed citizens of the state and enjoy many of the advantages of citizenship. But the state has exacted a high price for its benefits.

The most painful price to the Beduin is the forfeit of pride and honor due to their unofficial status as underprivileged recipients, expressed in that phrase *We give them*. To Westerners, this may seem a small price for the material benefits of modern living, but not to the Beduin. It seems to me that it is almost impossible for anyone who is not Beduin to grasp the significance of pride and honor in Beduin life, the depth to which these values inform the life and norms of Beduin society. Pride and the defense of honor enabled Beduin tribes to exist over the centuries in the harsh wilds of the desert, maintaining their independence not only from outside authorities but also within the constant tribal feuds that determined who would survive in the desert and who not. A tribe's strength was judged partly by the lengths to which it would go to defend its pride and honor and to retain its independence.

But however tangible pride and honor are for most Beduin, they are irrelevant to most Israeli Jews when they think of Beduin society. Where both Israeli Jews and Israeli Beduin do see eye to eye is on the tangible form of the price paid by the Beduin for citizenship—land.

Land has been the focus of conflict between nomads and settled people throughout the world in recent history. In Israel, some see it as the inevitable conflict between "the desert and the sown," between the wild imperative of the desert and the different rules and norms of settled culture. But the fate of the Plains Indians in the United States, of the aborigines of the Australian continent, or of the gypsies of Europe is all too similar to that of the Beduin now being enacted in the Middle East. They indicate that this is not a specifically desert problem, but one of modern civilization and its imperatives, its need for land, and its opposition to a

nomadic society's low-density use of rangeland. As centralized governments have gained power, so they have expropriated the land of native nomads, attempting to enforce their own
codes on those of fiercely independent people who inevitably,
for lack of power in a society whose rules they were slow to
grasp, succumbed to the bulldozer of "civilization."

The Beduin of the Middle East retained their fierce
independence well into the twentieth century. But the rapidly
changing picture of new nationalisms and new regimes in the
Middle East has taken a heavy toll on Beduin culture. In Arab
lands, the Beduin have been deprived of the basis of their
independence—land and the freedom to move on it. Both
Syria and Saudi Arabia nationalized Beduin rangelands in the
early 1950s. Syria organized the tribes into cooperatives,
settling them to work on what was formerly their own land.
They were not allowed even to buy the land that they
considered their own. Jordan introduced a law severely
limiting the range possibilities of the black goat—the main
herd animal of many Mideastern Beduin—by the simple
expedient of allowing only female goats to graze. Deeply
distrustful of the independence of the Beduin, and struggling
to enforce their authority in a notoriously unstable region, the
new regimes sought to curb the Beduin's independence,
seeing their tribal loyalties as a threat to centralized government. We know little of how these measures were carried out,
for there is no free flow of information within the Arab
countries, but it appears that it was done with a degree of
insensitivity and brutality at least equal to that used against
nomadic peoples elsewhere in the world.

Israel's record of treatment of its Beduin citizens was once
far better than that of its Arab neighbors. But it is now rapidly
deteriorating. The difference is that in Israel there is a free
flow of information. The details are known; the Beduin have
raised their voices. For Israel is a democratic state. And herein
lies the rub. As the only democracy in the Middle East, Israel
should surely not be resorting to the same methods and tactics

as its Arab neighbors. A democracy should surely be capable of dealing decently and justly with Beduin land claims, negotiating a solution to the satisfaction of all concerned. Admittedly, this may be expecting too much. Where the United States has failed with its Indian population, there is no reason to suppose that Israel would succeed with its Beduin population. And yet one cares far more deeply about the injustices perpetrated by one's own society, and I am thus deeply concerned about the situation of the Beduin in Israel.

Furthermore, the situation of the Israeli Beduin is far more complex than that of the American Indian. For the Beduin are Arabs. And Israel, despite the peace treaty with Egypt, is still on a war footing with the major part of the Arab world. This adds an important and especially painful dimension to the saga of the deteriorating relations between the Israeli authorities and Israeli Beduin.

Until 1948, when Israel conquered the Negev in its War of Independence, driving back an invasion by the Egyptian army, the Beduin were the only long-term inhabitants of this desert. Though the previous Turkish and British colonial regimes had both required formal land registration, they were very lax about enforcing it in the desert. And few Beduin wished to pay land taxes to a foreign occupier; they relied on their oral law and the tenancy of centuries to determine the boundaries of each tribe's land and of each family's land within the tribe.

Today, under Israeli law, formal registration documents are the only acceptable proof of land ownership. And the Beduin do not have them. The state of Israel has therefore claimed all the lands in the Negev that the Beduin regard as their own.

Before Israeli statehood, there were some sixty thousand Beduin in the Negev. Most fled to Jordan during the War of Independence, leaving only some thirteen thousand. The sheikhs of the remaining tribes met with Israel's then Chief-of-Staff Yigael Yadin (now Deputy Premier) and President Chaim Weizmann, and in return for an assurance that their lands would remain theirs, agreed to move into a reservation area in a triangle of the northeastern Negev for "a couple of years" for what were termed security reasons.

The couple of years lasted until 1966, when the military administration that governed all Israel's Arabs was finally abolished. But by that time, Jewish towns and villages had been built on several tracks of Beduin land, expropriated by the state. And the state now declared that the whole of the Negev was state property. The Beduin could return to their former lands as lessees, not as owners. Many refused to sign leases and returned illegally to their tribal lands.

Yet until the mid-seventies an uneasy status quo prevailed. The government did not act further on its claim of ownership other than to forbid the building of permanent housing on state lands. A laissez-faire policy developed under which the Beduin lived in a kind of temporary permanence. Meanwhile the Beduin proved themselves extraordinarily loyal to the state. They were part of the backbone of Israeli military security in the Negev in the first two decades of Israeli statehood, joining the regular army as trackers and commandos in territory with which they were far more familiar than Israeli Jews. Many among them paid for their service with injury and death in the Israeli-Arab wars.

The land dispute remained in abeyance, and there was still hope that it would be resolved. Contacts with the authorities were often very close. The Labor party, which held power in Israel from 1948 to 1977, created a special section for the Beduin, and in nearly every parliament since the inception of the state, there has been at least one Beduin member of the Knesset. Health, educational, and welfare services were provided on a scale that the Beduin had never encountered before. Compared to the Turkish and British predecessors, the Israelis had much to offer. Above all, they offered close contact with a modernizing society and an alternative to the traditional pastoral life of the Beduin.

As the years passed, the Negev Beduin began to look on

their flocks more as a means of insurance than as their main income. They worked in the army, in Jewish agricultural settlements, or in construction, and brought home higher salaries than ever before. Home, too, was very different. Instead of the traditional tent of the nomadic pastoral life, many Beduin now lived in shacks and huts. Forbidden to build permanent housing, they used any available materials—sheets of corrugated iron, cinder blocks, clay, canvas. These structures, interspersed with the goat-hair tents of tradition, now dot the northern Negev.

Meanwhile, though most Beduin still taught their children the pastoral way of life, some wise fathers saw to it that their children had a professional education. The issue of land ownership could not remain in abeyance forever, and a new professional elite of lawyers, doctors, and teachers began to agitate for a resolution to the dispute. The Labor government responded in the late sixties with a plan for six Beduin townships whose inhabitants would earn their living from industrial work in the Beersheba area. Two of these "industrial townships" were built. One, Tel Sheva, was acknowleged by the authorities as a planning and social disaster. The other, Shuval, is a success but is derided by most Beduin as for fellahin—peasant followers of the Beduin tribes—and not true Beduin. The remaining four townships never reached the drawing board.

By the mid-seventies, natural increase had tripled the Beduin population of Israel to some forty thousand. Alarmed at this growth and at the prospect of Beduin claims on over a fifth of the Negev, the Rabin government proposed a settlement in 1976. This proposal seemed, if not just, at least reasonable. The government could not acquiesce to such huge tracts of land as the Beduin claimed passing into private ownership; it therefore proposed that the Beduin receive compensation in alternate land for 20 percent of what they claimed, accept monetary compensation for a further 30 percent, and waive all claims to the remaining 50 percent. It was a deep insult to pride and honor, but it did satisfy the need for land. Or so it seemed at first glance. In fact, the settlement applied only to those Beduin who could prove ownership of the land—and few had the necessary registration documents. And although monetary compensation sounded generous, the assessed value of the land was minimal.

The sheikhs refused the proffered settlement. Honor demanded that the state formally recognize their title to their lands, and that they remain there. But they also refused to try to negotiate the terms of the offer, to a large degree because of faulty tribal leadership. The sheikhs, unable to trust one another, could present no united front or appeal to the government; moreover, their own cupidity often led them into personal deals with the authorities, ignoring the needs of their tribes. This point-blank refusal on their part heralded an era in which they would be subject to the full force of the existing law.

In January 1977, a new factor entered the picture with the formation of the "Green Patrol." This unit of a dozen men was accorded special police powers to ensure that the alarming number of Beduin goats and sheep in the Negev and in the north of the country, where they pastured during drought years, should cause no damage to agricultural settlements or to nature reserves. While the black goat is an integral part of the Negev ecosystem in reasonable numbers, the threefold increase in flocks over the past thirty years had made the animals a severe threat to the delicate desert vegetation, for the black goat will eat practically everything in sight. Thus the patrol's purpose seemed commendable at the time, and few questioned its formation. Indeed, few knew of it. It needed no formal cabinet approval, since its members were officially employees of the Nature Reserves Authority. The bulk of the patrol's budget, however, came from the Israel Lands Administration and the Ministry of Agriculture.

This was the situation in May 1977, when Menahem Begin's Likud government came to power. The new minister of agriculture was Ariel (Arik) Sharon, a brilliant general and wild civilian whose harsh and sudden evacuation of Beduin in northern Sinai in the early seventies and support of unauthorized settlers on the West Bank of the Jordan River had proved that he regarded the whole country as his own personal vision of the Wild West, where deeds speak far louder than law. Indeed, this man had single-handedly practically torpedoed the peace talks between Egypt and Israel early in 1978, when, as the talks were in progress, he set up unauthorized "posts" in northern Sinai.

Under Sharon's guidance, the Green Patrol now moved in to enforce every law at its disposal with the utmost rigor. There was practically no part of the Negev in which Beduin could graze their flocks without being culpable under one of some forty laws and regulations ranging from trespassing to veterinary laws. Black goats caught by the Green Patrol were sent immediately for slaughter, and sheep were held in "quarantine" until the police finished drawing up charges against the Beduin trespassers—a form of fiscal punishment that amounted in some cases to thousands of dollars.

Within a few months, the Green Patrol became a curse word among the Beduin. Stories of its brutality and misuse of the law, let alone plain harassment, were rife. Green Patrol operatives pointed out that the complainants could always take them to court; the Beduin replied that they were scared to do so for fear of recriminations. Meanwhile, formal government expropriation of land in the Negev for military and industrial purposes was stepped up, and Beduin living in illegal shacks and tents on the land were evacuated—back into the former reservation area. The new policy, as stated by an Israel Lands Administration official, was "to sever the link between the Beduin and the land." Moving them back into the reservation area was only the first stage. The second stage would be the establishment of the old Labor plan for six "industrial villages," into which all of the Beduin would be moved.

The head of the Green Patrol is Alon Galili, a short, burly, moustachioed man in his early forties. He has dark dancing eyes and a forearm the size of which convinces you that he could knock you out with one sideswipe. When I first approached him about going out with the Green Patrol to see exactly how they worked, he tried to dissuade me. "This isn't pleasant work," he said. "But it has to be done. You really don't want to know about it."

I replied that I did and told him why.

"Listen," he said. "Get one thing straight. There's no such thing as justice in this world. One man's justice is another man getting screwed. That's it. Now there's one thing I'll fight for to the ends of this earth. And that's that this land remain ours, Jewish. Land that we bought in the Negev with blood and money is ours. It was the Beduin's before? Fine. It's ours now."

Galili is a firm opponent of the proposed 1976 land arrangement, voicing his opposition to it with the deliberate choice of the coarsest expression in which he seems to delight. "That was a ridiculously large offer. The government was tearing the crotch of its pants in its attempt to be generous."

So what, I asked, does he want to see happen with the Beduin?

"I want order. That's all. Order. The laws exist, and they should be made to work. The Beduin are citizens of the state, so they must abide by its laws. They didn't choose to be citizens? That's too bad. You're talking justice, and there isn't any. Now policy is just not my business; my business is simply to enforce the law. And in any case, to make policy you first have to have order. And that's what we're doing in the Green Patrol—making order."

I asked in what context they are making order. "Oh, everyone comes to us," said Galili. "Why? Because they know we're the only ones who can get things done. Nothing can be done around here, in the Negev, without my knowing about it. My boys are strong and tough, and they do the job. For instance, when Beduin kids were throwing stones at the train to the phosphate works near the Dead Sea, Israel Railways came to me. So we gathered together the heads of the families living around there, and said 'Out.' They got out of the area."

But why did Israel Railways go to him instead of to the police?

"You should ask the police that one. But the truth is that the police are fat and can't move. My boys are lean and know the score. And if the Beduin don't want to move when we say 'Move,' then we just fold up their tents ourselves and wait until they move." And so saying, Galili folded his arms and sat back with a grin, indicating how he waits. Finally, after many false starts, he consented to my accompanying the Green Patrol on an "operation" in the central Negev.

Galili's boys were indeed lean and tough. They were nearly all in their early twenties, and took evident delight in the pistols prominently displayed on their hips and in the sirens on their specially outfitted jeeps. I was interested in one patrol member in particular—a good-looking, baby-faced young man with a charming smile and high spirits, called Momo. Most of the stories of Green Patrol brutality involved Momo, and at first it was hard to understand why—until I saw him get angry. He had taken insult at something an old Beduin man had said. No sooner were the words out of the old man's mouth—meant, as far as I could tell, in all innocence—than Momo went red. In an instant, that baby face contorted into ugliness: his lips curled, his nose sharpened, his whole head hunched down between his shoulders and thrust forward in anger. He seized the old man by the arm and shook him. "What the hell are you talking about?" he screamed. "Are you calling me a liar? Are you? Are you?"

Glancing toward me, Galili intervened, pulling Momo away from the old man. Ten minutes later the old man had apologized to Momo, and Momo was smiling again.

That day, we had met at five in the morning near Sde Boker, in the central Negev. Three jeeps were to wait in radio contact with a fourth, driven by Momo, which would scout out illegal flocks. I jumped onto the fourth jeep. There were six of us in it. When we spotted a flock, we would contact the others and the jeeps would close in on the flock from all directions. We drove out into the mountains west of Mitzpe Ramon, where Momo was determined to catch a woman who regularly watered her flock in cisterns nearby but who had always evaded him when he'd given chase. "Today we're going to get her," he declared with satisfaction. "She's gotten away from me once too often. Today she's going to pay for it."

It was rough terrain, and soon we had to leave the jeeps and go by foot. After a while, we found a trail of fresh sheep droppings. The flock had passed perhaps an hour before. We went faster and split into three pairs. Each pair would go up to a high point and look around. "Whoever spots her first fires two shots in the air," said Momo. We separated, and I went with him.

Ten minutes later, I spotted the flock on a distant hillside, moving rapidly away from us. I said nothing. A moment later, Momo also spotted them, and shouting in delight, fired his gun. Answering shots came from the hills around, and soon all six of us were racing over the stony ground. But the Beduin woman knew this terrain far better than we, and was soon well over two miles away from us. Disgusted and winded, Momo signaled to turn back. He and I walked ahead of the others as he muttered in anger at having lost the flock. Suddenly a bullet whined past my ear. I wheeled around with a "What the hell. . . ."

And I saw Razi, one of the four some twenty yards behind us, giggling as he struggled to get his pistol into his holster. He waved his hand at me. "Safety catch isn't too good on this gun," he shouted.

From then on, I made sure to walk behind Razi.

When we got back to the jeep we contacted Galili and reported that we'd lost the flock. Momo suggested we go after another one that often grazed high up above Ein Akev, a perennial spring some miles away from Sde Boker. Galili gave the okay. We drove north, and five of us left the jeep. Again, the only way to get to the area was to walk. When I mentioned that it seemed a rather reckless thing to do when we had no water bottles with us, Momo assured me that the flock was only a couple of miles away. In fact, we were to walk fast for three hours without water as the morning sun increased in heat.

Razi and Momo walked on either side of me at first, both of them wearing the orange T-shirt of the Nature Reserves Authority, printed with the authority's emblem, a gazelle's head. As we walked, Momo told me of a trip he was planning to the States, Razi of a farm he wanted to start. We were covering some of the most beautiful terrain in the Negev, but perhaps they had seen too much of it, for they paid no attention. Soon they tired of plans for the future and began to swap information as to the best jeep for this part of the world. From jeeps, it seemed but a short jump to guns, and soon they were vying with each other to come up with the best gun for various conditions. Momo's favorite, he explained, was one "that will drop a gazelle at a distance of fifty yards." There seemed little point in my reminding employees of the Nature Reserves Authority that the gazelle was a legally protected species in Israel.

By the time we reached Ein Akev, we were all exhausted and dehydrated. We had zigzagged over the area, following the grazing pattern of a flock of sheep and goats that—judging from their droppings—had been there the day before. Just as we came onto the cliffs above the spring, where we could see the glimmer of water far down in the ravine below, Momo spotted a goat high up on a crag above us. "Come on," he yelled. "There they are!" The rest of us stood stock still in amazement as Momo, who must have been as dehydrated and giddy as we, went racing up the rocks after the goat. Convinced that he could not keep up the chase at that pace for more than half a mile, we scrambled down to the spring, where we drank and rested in the shade of the rocks. The next thing we knew, we were surrounded by sheep and goats, followed by Momo and Galili victoriously urging them forward with sticks and shouts. Momo was reeling, and grinning beatifically.

Behind them ran an old man and two women, one very old, one much younger. The young woman kept clutching at Galili, screaming and shouting at him. He ignored her. Momo told us how he had radioed Galili for help, and how Galili had raced up the sides of the ravine to help head off part of the flock while the Beduin shepherds sped off in the opposite direction with the rest of it. "At last five hundred head," said Momo. "Two hundred head, for god's sake," said Galili.

We all walked down the ravine together, driving the captured part of the flock, mostly goats, before us. They had drunk from the spring earlier that morning, and their sides were swollen with the water in their bellies. The younger woman went from one to the other of us, begging us to let the goats go, to let her be, to have pity on her aging father, whom we had left by the spring. He had simply refused to move. Behind us, the old woman walked silently, bent over her stick, her face creased into a mass of wrinkles, so that the indigo dye of the tattoos of her youth were barely distinguishable among them. She walked barefoot. Her daughter wore plastic sandals.

At the bottom of the ravine, the rest of the Green Patrol was waiting for us, together with a truck for the goats. An impromptu pen had been prepared, and the patrol men herded the goats into the pen, then began to throw them up into the truck backed up to it. The goats would be sold for slaughter that afternoon and the money from the sale held in trust until the case came up in court. The court would then decide how much to deduct for expenses before awarding the remainder back to the shepherds.

When the truck was half full, the old woman suddenly came to life. Screaming that they would kill her goats by throwing them onto the truck like that, she jumped up onto it. As it filled up, she moved to the front, weeping and wailing, one thin bare arm hooked through the struts of the truck's side as she fought for balance among the jostling animals. The patrol men piled seventy goats onto the truck; no more could possibly fit in. But the old woman refused to come down. She wouldn't leave her goats. Galili began to plead with her, then to shout at her. Her only answer was louder weeping and wailing until finally she agreed to come down if he would let the rest of the goats and the few sheep go and allow her to pick out the five best goats to be taken off the truck.

She came down and picked out the five goats. The patrol men slammed shut the tailgate of the truck, and it began to move off along the dusty track through the hills. And as it did so, the old woman let out a horrible wail. She was standing on a slight rise between where I stood and the moving truck. And now, as the truck moved off down the trail, she held out her right hand high in the air, mutely imploring the truck to stop. As it began to pick up speed, she started running down the rise after it. Arm still upraised, that black-shrouded figure gradually disappeared from view as she descended the rise—first the feet, then the legs, then back, shoulders, and head, until all that was left in view was the sight of the dust billowing up on the trail behind the truck, and all that was to be heard was the occasional bleat of a goat wafted back down the trail on the breeze. In that one minute, it seemed, I had been witness to the whole sad tale of a disappearing culture.

I had seen no open violence during my time with the Green Patrol. But I was still haunted by stories told by Beduin of Green Patrol tactics: driving through Beduin encampments shooting dogs at random; driving an old man fifty miles away from his home and leaving him alone at night in the desert to make his way back as best he could; holding guns to children's heads as their parents were ordered to pull down their tents. In one well-documented operation in April 1978, Green Patrol men together with personnel of the Israel Lands Administration descended on a Beduin encampment in the northeastern Negev, reportedly without warning, tore down tents and several cinder-block huts, and trucked them together with their contents several miles away, where they dumped everything in a huge pile in the middle of a Beduin cemetery. The owner of one of those tents was Juammar el-Ativa, a tracker who had served in the Israel Defense Forces for six years. "Until now I've served faithfully in the army," he said in shock. "But now I don't know if I can continue."

The legal justification for that operation, as for many of the demolition operations against Beduin property, was questionable. Five months before, the finance minister had signed an order slating the land for military industries. The notice was published two months later in the official government gazette, and the mandatory period of two months declared for objections. But the sheikh of the tribe living on the land received a copy of this notice only after another three months had passed—a month too late to file an objection. Demolition orders had already been approved, and before the Beduin could appeal, the bulldozers, trucks, and jeeps had arrived. The Beduin were not even allowed to remove personal possessions from the huts and tents.

Even when appeals against such orders have been filed, demolitions have still been carried out. District court orders have been sidestepped several times. In April 1979, a promise of stay of execution on an evacuation order, made by the deputy attorney general to Beduin representatives before the high court, was ignored. Government bulldozers were sent in to prepare the ground, tearing down newly planted vineyards. Old people and children in the encampment stoned the workmen, who backed down but returned the next day with a police escort to meet another barrage of stones and violence in which several Beduin, workmen, and policemen were hurt. The younger men of the area were not present: they had all been called into the nearest police station that morning for questioning on suspected terrorist activities. A coincidence, explained the police. A planned diversion, said the Beduin, intended to place in public question their loyalty to the state.

The high court angrily accused the authorities of "a disgusting act of contempt of court" and ordered the responsible official brought before it, stating that "he may be jailed." The high court's protest was scheduled for immediate debate in both the cabinet and the Knesset. But it was debated in neither, since both cabinet and Knesset accepted the opinion of the attorney general that the case was sub judice, even though both were scheduled to debate not the case itself, but the statements of the high court on the government's behavior. It was a dangerous precedent of the Knesset—the legislature—abiding by the judgment of the executive as to its scope of discussion and action.

The high court, meanwhile, o: iered the attorney general to investigate the affair. Two weeks later, the attorney general apologized to the court on behalf of the government and recommended disciplinary action against seven senior government officials, including the head of the Israel Lands Administration's Beersheba office and the director of the southern district of the Ministry of the Interior. He also ordered an investigation into the possibility of criminal collusion on the part of the local police. (Six months later, no disciplinary proceedings had been instituted, and the investigation of the police was still in progress.)

The fact that the men of the area were questioned by the police that April day was a symptom of another disturbing development in the government's attitude to its Beduin citizens. After the Begin government came to power in 1977, stories began to circulate in the media presenting the Beduin as a menace to the general welfare of the state. The Beduin were cutting down trees and hunting gazelles, it was reported; they were breaking water pipes and wasting water; they were defrauding national insurance, endangering public health, and taking possession of the land in an attempt to "encircle the cities." These activities, it was said, were being encouraged and financed by Israel's enemies—by the Palestine Liberation Organization, by Libya, and by Saudi Arabia. Alon Galili claimed that "we have recently discovered that the movement of Beduin and their flocks on Israeli land is not innocent. There is a hand guiding them from Saudi Arabia or from Jordan, telling them where to spread out, and dividing Israel up into plots of land. This invisible hand sees to it that each Beduin moves toward some Jewish plot of land."

"None of this is true," says Nuri el-Aukbi, an activist for Beduin rights. "We're not trying to take over land. We're quite willing to live in a Jewish state. There is room for both of us, Beduin and Jews. We're not saying they should give us the whole country, but just that small part of it that is ours, so that we can farm it and live off it honorably." El-Aukbi advocates what the majority of the Beduin now want—a compromise solution by which the Beduin would receive enough land to enable them to set up cooperative agricultural settlements, known in Israel as *moshavim*.

The Association for Civil Rights in Israel—a liberal, nonpartisan group of concerned Jewish academics and jurists—has made a detailed study of constructive alternatives to the government plan for six "industrial townships," charging that the planned townships "totally lack any economic foundation and are meant only to provide living quarters for a labor force." Dr. Clinton Bailey, chairman of the association and an anthropologist specializing in Beduin affairs, estimates that 70 percent of the Negev Beduin would find *moshavim* an equitable way to move from their traditional mode of life into a modern society, while still retaining their link to the land. The Beduin could be as successful in *moshavim* as Jewish

settlers were in northern Sinai, he argues, where the heat of
the desert and advanced agricultural technology were used to
produce out-of-season export flowers, fruits, and vegetables.
Five hundred Beduin families have had a standing request in
to the Ministry of Agriculture for the past three years,
applying for permission to start five *moshavim* in the Negev.
Their request has simply been ignored, and the present
government has not even commented on the study submitted
by the Association for Civil Rights.

For months, unwilling to admit the full meaning of what I
was seeing and hearing, I sought an answer to why the
government was being so hardheaded, denying the Beduin
either any alternative to the industrial townships or even the
basic right of being consulted as to their own future. I received
an unequivocal answer in an interview with a senior government official directly involved with the issue at the time. It
was this interview that convinced me that the main stumbling
block to Israel being able to deal fairly and decently with its
Beduin citizens was a matter neither of "desert and sown" nor
of "primitive versus civilized society," but of the ugly
reverberations within Israel of the Arab-Israeli conflict.

We began by discussing the plan for the industrial townships, which were indicated on a map in the official's office as
six big, bright pink circles ranged around the Beersheba area.
After a while, disturbed at the single-minded commitment to
what appeared to be a very vague plan, I said: "You know, it
disturbs me that in all this thinking about the industrial
townships, you seem to be allowing no alternative."

"What do you mean?"

"Well, it seems to me that the situation is one in which you
are saying to the Beduin, 'Either you do what we want you to
do, or we force you to do it.' You want all the Beduin to go
into the industrial townships. But the Beduin themselves have
other ideas. For instance, the majority, according to one
survey, want some form of agricultural future, such as
moshavim. This idea has been brought up several times and

always rejected by the government authorities concerned. Why?"

The moment I mentioned the word *moshavim*, a radical change came over the calm official sitting across the desk from me. He sat up in his chair, quite red in the face, leaned across the desk toward me, and, banging his fist on the desk top said, "Of course that idea has been rejected. Quite rightly. *Moshavim!* We should give good agricultural land to the Beduin? The Jews do agriculture far better than the Beduin, and the Jews will have the *moshavim*, not the Beduin." It was at this point in the interview that he first insisted that I could not use his name, a condition he stressed repeatedly as we went on talking.

"But the Beduin can learn the new techniques of desert agriculture as easily as the Jews."

"Listen to me. The Beduin are human material that is the antithesis of order. And you need order to establish *moshavim*. We want that land for the Jews! Every inch of land is now of vital importance for the future of the country. The Jews of Israel need the land; that land belongs to the state, and the state will give it to the Jews to work. And the state will decide, not the Beduin, where the Beduin will live and what they will do."

"But as Israeli citizens, surely the Beduin have the right to choose what kind of life they want to live and where, just as do Israeli Jews?"

"They can choose."

"You mean you *are* considering an alternative?"

"I mean they can choose. Of course they can choose. They can stay where they are with their flocks outside the reservation area, and the Green Patrol will come along every day and confiscate their goats and take their sheep off to the quarantine station and bring trespassing charges against them. But they can keep on like that if they want. Of course they have a choice. To keep on like that or to go into an industrial township. What do you think they want *moshavim* for? They want the land, that's why—land and water. Well, I'm not going to give it to them."

"What about the offer of a land settlement made by the previous government?"

"I would never have made such an offer. The percentages are far too high. But in any case, the response from the Beduin makes the whole thing a farce."

"Surely that's because they can't prove ownership under Israeli law."

"So it's not their land. It belongs to the state. If they can't claim it legally, then it's clear who the land belongs to. These six townships are the maximum of what I have to offer—maybe another township or two, but that's it. There are two possible options for settling the Beduin—agriculture and industry—and I've decided that they'll work in industry. If they had *moshavim* they'd only start spreading out, slowly annexing more and more land to their settlements. All they want is our land. And in any case there's no water to give them."

"There's water to give to the twenty Jewish agricultural settlements now being built in the northwestern Negev."

"The water is only for Jewish settlements. I'm not giving it to Arabs."

The look on my face must have showed him how far he had gone. "Look," he said, changing his tone abruptly to one of paternal comfort, "I can see that it's hard for you to face up to the political realities we're dealing with. It may not be pleasant, but in the long run it's the best for everyone, including the Beduin."

"Aren't you worried that the Beduin will become embittered by such a policy?" I asked.

"So, they'll be bitter for twenty or thirty years. So what? After that they'll forget all about it."

Only a few months later, the government took a step that ensured that the Negev Beduin would never "forget about it." It was the latest blow in the increasingly bitter and even violent struggle between the Beduin and the authorities since Menahem Begin's Likud government came to power in 1977.

The Negev Lands Purchase (Peace Agreement with Egypt) Law was presented to Israel's parliament in July 1979 by the government. Under it, the state could expropriate Beduin-occupied land without court orders. The law, as tabled in the Knesset, specified 157,000 acres in the northeastern Negev, but included a paragraph stating that at the discretion of the defense minister and the defense and foreign affairs committee of parliament, this area could be enlarged to any size required within a total area covering all of the Negev and parts of the hill country to the north of it.

The government explained that it needed the land for a joint military and civilian airfield, planned long before the peace treaty with Egypt, but now to be built by April 1982, the final date for Israel's withdrawal of its armed forces from Sinai. Because of the tight timetable of the peace treaty, said government officials, there was no time for normal expropriation procedures; in this case, the security factor took precedence and required a special law. The airfield (one of three to be built in the Negev by the 1982 deadline, with the other two being built by American firms and labor) was vital to Israel's security, and work had to start immediately, they said. Alternatives to the law, such as establishing a special judicial commission to expedite regular expropriation procedures and appeals, were not explored.

The new bill was basically an ultimatum to the Beduin, allowing no negotiations and, since the courts would have no jurisdiction under it, denying the right of appeal to close to ten thousand Beduin citizens living in the 157,000 acres specified for immediate expropriation. The bill did allow for compensation, but on a minimal level: a maximum of one acre of agricultural land (i.e., land with water supply) for the few large, Beduin landowners, or an alternative 20 percent of their land without water supply—again, only for the largest land-owners. The only viable alternative left to most Beduin under the new bill was to move into one of the four new "industrial townships" provided for in the bill—and as yet unbuilt, since the land for them was itself to be expropriated from the Beduin under the new bill.

The bitterness accumulating among the Beduin over the previous two years now reached a peak. Dr. Yunis Abu-Rabiya, a respected Beduin physician in Beersheba, called the law racist, pointing out that it applied to only one ethnic group. "How can a country that calls itself democratic deny the elementary citizen's right of appeal to the courts?" he asked. Activist Nuri el-Aukbi commented acerbicly: "If we were Jews, the government would never dream of such a law."

As though to underscore his accusation, in the same week that the new bill was tabled in the Knesset, the government began high-level negotiations with Jewish settlers in Sinai over alternative housing and compensation. (They will have to leave their homes as a result of the peace treaty, since the whole of Sinai will return to Egypt.) But the variety of options and the sums of money under discussion were poles apart from the terms established for the Beduin by the new bill. For instance, the settlers of Moshav Neot Sinai have already received $800,000 for the one-hundred-acre vegetable garden returned to Egypt in June 1979 in the first phase of Israel's withdrawal from Sinai. Most of this garden was still uncultivated. By comparison, a Beduin family of eight people with fifty acres of land would receive an absolute maximum of $14,185—or a mere 3 percent of what the Moshav Neot Sinai people received for similar land.

Under heavy attack from the opposition Labor party when the bill came up for its first reading in parliament, the government agreed to cancel the paragraph allowing it to expand the area to be expropriated at its own discretion, to allow court appeal over compensation—though not over expropriation—and to delay the second and third readings of the bill, negotiating with the Beduin for voluntary evacuation of the land meanwhile. The quid pro quo was a Labor promise to vote for the bill in its final readings.

More than any other single move, this bill seems to have drawn the Beduin into clearly aligning themselves within the Mideast conflict. Formerly, they had considered themselves outside that conflict, a people apart. Called Beduin only by outsiders, they called themselves *el-Arab*, *the* Arab, since they were the elite of the Arab peoples, the ones who had spread the word of Muhammad throughout the Middle East. They looked down on other Arabs as other Arabs looked down on them. Now that has changed. In demonstrations against the new bill, Israeli Arabs from the Galilee in the north of the country, who have been fighting an increasingly bitter battle for land in the last few years, outnumbered the Beduin with whom they were demonstrating solidarity. Inevitably, identification with the cause of other Israeli Arabs and with the Palestinian issue in general is increasing among the Beduin, especially the young, educated elite. Beduin lawyer Khalil Abu-Rabiya drew the comparison. "The Beduin will be a refugee on his own land," he said. "He won't be over the border dreaming of his homeland like the Palestinians; he'll be here, living here, going to work on a conveyor belt every day in a factory built on what was his land, established on the expropriation of his rights."

But unless the government were to concede the issue of agricultural settlements, one important factor will still differentiate the Beduin from other Israeli Arabs or Palestinians. As far as the Beduin are concerned, they are still *el-Arab*, and not Palestinians. And thus they do not have what the Palestinians now have: hope. In the past few years, the Palestinian identity of most of Israel's Arab population appears to have strengthened; in the event of a comprehensive Middle East peace, they might gain a strong identity on which to base their role in the area. But for the Negev Beduin, the still far-off days of Arab-Israeli peace offer no hope. For theirs is a small and dying civilization. Their traditions and customs have been gradually fading beyond memory over the last thirty years. In the planned "industrial townships," this civilization would altogether disappear. It now seems that by the time there is peace, and distrust between Jew and Arab begins to dissipate as a result of it, the Beduin will have been long buried in the industrial subculture of the northern Negev . . . and in the yellowing volumes of archives and libraries.

13 · Peace

In spring 1978, when I began working on this book, I decided to write this last chapter on the effects of an Israeli-Egypt peace treaty on the Sinai and the Negev. At that time, such a decision was an act of faith. Egyptian President Anwar Sadat's dramatic visit to Jerusalem in November 1977 already seemed to belong to the far-off world of legend. The euphoria and high hopes of those three dramatic days in Jerusalem and the month that followed them had faded, and peace seemed almost as ephemeral as it had been before the Sadat visit. But it had been tantalizingly close. And if we had come so close before, I thought, we could surely do so again.

Just one year later, this chapter was no longer an act of faith, but one of realistic appraisal. The peace treaty between Egypt and Israel was signed on March 26, 1979. By 1982, Israel will have withdrawn all its armed forces from the Sinai, and the border between Egypt and Israel will again run, as it did prior to 1967, along the line drawn by the Turks and the British in 1906, the political line that divides the Sinai from the Negev. But this time, that border will be open. For the first time in recorded history, it seems that the Sinai will become a desert of peace.

For the Sinai, peace is tantamount to a revolution. For not only is this the holiest desert in the world, it is also the most fought-for desert in the world. No other desert has claimed so much awe, and so much blood. Major C. S. Jarvis, the military governor of Sinai under the British High Commissioner in Egypt in the 1920s and 1930s, reckoned that armies had advanced and retreated over this desert no less than forty-five times. Since his administration, four more times have been added to this desert's tally of death. Few men in Israel or Egypt do not know at least some of the long list of names of desert battlefields. And even the most casual traveler in the sand dunes of the northern Sinai notices the odd tank tracks jutting out of the sand here, the yards of barbed wire trailing along a dune there. As the dunes shift with each sandstorm, they uncover anew the remnants of battle—a boot, the flesh that was in it long rotted away; bones, pitted and bleached by sand and sun; and always, more tank tracks, more charred remains of military vehicles, more barbed wire.

Yet it was out of war that peace was born; specifically, out of what the Israelis call the Yom Kippur War of 1973, and the Egyptians, the Ramadan War—for both peoples fought through the holiest days of their calendars. This holy desert, the Sinai, it seems, would demand that. Out of the carnage of that war, the diplomats began to establish the basis for peace, first with the separation of forces agreement in 1974, and then with the interim agreement of 1975, which went into effect in February 1976. Under this agreement, a large swathe of the Sinai arching up from the Suez Canal became a United Nations buffer zone. And in that buffer zone, Israeli and Egyptian officers began to talk to each other of the possibility of peace.

In the fall of 1978, a month after the Camp David accords had been signed by President Sadat, Premier Begin, and President Carter, heralding the peace treaty to be signed seven months later, two army officers met in the buffer zone, as they had done regularly for the past three years. Both were in their late thirties. They were not close friends. They had never visited each other's homes. Nor could they, for one was Egyptian, the other Israeli. They were the officers in charge of the "population transfers" through the buffer zone, in which students would pass from Israeli-held territory to Egypt to continue their studies, and people would pass one way or the other to join up with their families for a few weeks or months before returning to work again "on the other side."

Under the eyes of the suntanned young Swedish United Nations soldiers manning that part of the zone, the two officers delayed as long as they could to chat. They talked in Arabic, which the Israeli knew fluently, though the Egyptian was fast learning Hebrew. And at this, their first meeting after the Camp David accords, they talked of peace. For at Camp David, the euphoric days of the Sadat visit to Jerusalem had returned. Peace was once more a tangible hope, almost a reality.

"Tell me," said the Israeli, "do you think this peace will be a real one? Can we really have true peace, so quickly, after all that has happened?"

The Egyptian looked him quietly in the eye awhile and lit a cigarette as he reflected on his answer. And then slowly, painfully, he answered: "I led the commando landing force at Ras Sudar in October 1973. Most of my men were killed; the rest and myself taken prisoner. I was a prisoner for fifty-four days, most of those days in an Israeli hospital. I was treated well. The doctors were excellent, the nurses kind. But I was still wounded; my men were still dead. Yes, the Camp David accords are excellent. But peace is not possible, not in our generation, not as long as there are people of our age who have fought and been wounded and seen their friends die, as you and I have. Camp David and the treaty that will now follow it are important as symbols. They are what will make real peace possible in the future. But they themselves are not peace. As Sadat once said, for our generation that's impossible. But now we are making it possible for the next generation, giving them the framework on which to build real peace within the next twenty or thirty years."

The Israeli nodded slowly in agreement. They turned to watch the line of travelers boarding the buses for Egypt and for Israel, then smiled at each other and exchanged the small tokens that had become part of the ritual of their meetings. A copy of the latest edition of Egypt's *October* magazine for the Israeli; color snapshots of the Israeli's family for the Egyptian. And as the dunes became golden under the dying sun, they turned each to his own jeep and set out on the long trip back home.

Yet despite the memories of the wounded and the dead, this encounter itself was peace. The Egyptian was right: it was not the "real peace" that they both sought, for they met as army officers, not as civilian friends. Yet here was the embryo of peace, the basis that would make the signatures on accords and treaties into a living reality. And if these two officers could talk in this way just five years after the deadliest war yet between Egypt and Israel had been fought over these very dunes, then it seemed to me that it would take far less than one generation for this embryo to develop into the maturity of "real peace."

Yet I understand the Egyptian officer's reticence very well, as did his Israeli counterpart. All three of us welcome the treaty wholeheartedly, in all its terms. And yet, after over thirty years of enmity and bloodshed, it is still hard to believe. The thought that in a short time those color snapshots will translate into living, smiling people for the Egyptian, or that *October* magazine will be on sale on Israeli newsstands—these are ideas that seem almost as incredible as the signing of the treaty itself. Time and again, I have to repeat to myself that the Sinai will still be open to me, even though it will once more be part of Egypt. I have to persuade myself of what I know to be true—that I will be able to go down to Santa Katerina and climb the mountains of the southern Sinai once more, as I have in the past; that I will be able to sit once again in the spring of Ein Gedeirat in the northern Sinai and watch the Beduin women as they wash their clothes in the gushing water and chatter and giggle in the shade.

But peace, too, has its price. Not nearly so heavy as that of death and injury, but painful all the same. For as Egyptians and Israelis struggle over the next few years to add the rapprochement of the present and the hope of the future to the memories of the past, the Sinai and the Negev, the desert over which they have fought so bitterly in that past, will change irrevocably.

For most of those who live in the Sinai, the peace treaty has brought with it hope and anxiety. But for some, such as the five thousand Israelis who have made their homes there since 1967, it means a bitter parting. They leave with a deep sense of betrayal by their own government, which urged them to settle there after 1967 and then, just twelve years later, ordered them to move out. They went there for what were termed "security reasons." By establishing an Israeli civilian population in various parts of the Sinai, the government reasoned, it would ensure that a certain normalization take place that would secure its hold on the peninsula. Now the best security of all—peace—has materialized. Yet the Israeli settlers are distrustful and suspicious. They leave behind them two small townships—Ophira at Sharm el Sheikh, near the southern tip of the peninsula, and Yamit on the northwestern coast—plus over twenty agricultural settlements, most of them in the northwestern Sinai in the Yamit area. And though they will be well compensated financially by the Israeli government for their relocation into Israel proper, they complain bitterly that they were used as pawns in the diplomatic bargaining process of peace.

Some residents of the Sinai are sorry to see the Israelis go. The people of El Arish, the shantytown on the northwest coast that is the "capital" of the Sinai, welcomed the return to Egyptian sovereignty in May 1979, but have good memories of their twelve years under Israeli rule. The Israelis brought electricity to El Arish, radically changing the lives of the townspeople and preparing the way for modernization. Now this town on the southeastern Mediterranean coast is planning a future as a tourist center, capitalizing on its palm-studded white sands and calm sea. Its first hotel has opened, though hardly a five-star affair, and it is preparing to be the way station on the main tourist road through the Sinai from Cairo to Tel Aviv.

The Sinai's twenty-five thousand Beduin have mixed feelings about peace. In the southern Sinai in particular, the Beduin are anxious lest some Egyptian officials, in the spirit of the past rather than that of peace, take steps against them for having cooperated with the Israelis since 1967. It was a close and friendly cooperation. In striking contrast to the story of the Beduin in the Negev, the Israeli occupation of the southern Sinai was a boon for the local Beduin. There were no clashes over land claims in the southern Sinai, and the Beduin found their life-style and desert lore respected by the new occupiers. Where they had been ignored under the Egyptian government, they now found Israeli officials and army personnel who took a personal interest in helping them, pushing through small-scale medical, educational, and housing projects that gradually changed the Beduins' perception of the world. In Santa Katerina and at Firan, for example, small housing units made out of local materials, designed and built by the Israelis and the Beduin together, blend easily into the landscape. Through Israeli archaeologists, scientists, and administrative personnel, the Beduin found work that paid higher wages than they had ever received before, and, more important still, allowed the menfolk to stay with their families instead of spending up to ten months a year, as they used to do, across the Suez Canal, returning only to see their families briefly and give them their wages. Now many Beduin fear that they will have to cross the canal once again to find work and that their new prosperity will disappear as quickly as it came.

Some of the Beduin of the northwestern Sinai are less mixed in their reactions, for it was here that General Arik Sharon, now minister of agriculture but in the early seventies still O/C Southern Command, brutally and high-handedly herded the Beduin out of the area south of the Gaza Strip to evacuate the land for Israeli settlements. Many of the Beduin here will be glad to see the Israelis go, but since the Egyptians will come in their stead to the same towns and settlements, they fear that they will never get back their lands.

But perhaps the greatest anxiety about peace is felt by the Greek Orthodox monks of Santa Katerina Monastery, at the foot of Mount Sinai. This tiny fortress houses some twenty monks, guest accommodations, a church, a mosque (built as protection against Moslem invaders, who are forbidden to fight within forty paces of a mosque), four wells, an ossiary, workshops, a library, and one of the world's most stunning collections of Byzantine icons, which the monastery managed to preserve during the iconoclastic era simply because it was so isolated from the rest of the Byzantine Empire that it could take the risk of ignoring orders from the north to destroy its treasures. Beneath the present buildings, there is a veritable maze of hidden, walled-up, and forgotten rooms and cellars in which such treasures as the Codex Sinaiticus, the earliest known version of the Bible, have been found.

Since the sixth century, when Emperor Justinian built Santa Katerina to afford protection against raiders for the hermits and monks of the area, the monastery has been the center of a large feudal fiefdom in the southern Sinai, claiming the special loyalty of the Jebeliya tribe of Beduin, who take their name from *Jebel*, the "Mount": Mount Sinai. The many strange details about the monastery—the existence of what is in effect a tiny Greek village within the wilds of Sinai; the discovery that the burning bush against which the main chapel is built is actually a raspberry bush (the red berries represent flames); the realization that Mount Sinai is not the highest mountain in the southern Sinai range—are compounded by the history of the Jebeliya Beduin. Originally, they were not even Arabs, but Wallachian peasants shipped from Europe by Justinian to act as servants for the monks in the new monastery. Within a century, they had converted to Islam and intermarried with local Beduin tribes until they became, to all intents and purposes, Beduin, the only remnants of their European past being the flowered bonnets worn by their young girls and the strikingly east-European bone structure beneath the dark olive skin of some of the men. But though the centuries changed their religion, their clothing, and their language, they did not change the Beduins' loyalty to the monastery, which was their main source of income. They acted and still act as its guards and its gardeners, and farm the small orchards in the ravines around the monastery, offering half their produce to the monks and keeping half for themselves.

The archbishop of Santa Katerina, the center of a bishopric that includes monasteries in E-Tur near Suez, in Cyprus, and in Egypt itself, is still the main authority of the area, even though that authority was sorely challenged by the Israelis. While there have always been pilgrims coming to Santa Katerina, there was never a flood of tourists such as after the Israelis took over in 1967. By 1979 the monastery was staggering under the flood of visitors, up from maybe ten a week before 1967 to peaks of three or four hundred a week. It was a profitable business, since the monastery charges admission fees and sells pamphlets and postcards. But Archbishop Damianos, the leader of the community for the last ten years, felt that it was also a degrading one. As we sat in his comfortably appointed reception room within the monastery, its walls hung with tapestries and photographs, and sipped coffee, he mourned the changes that were threatening his area.

"We monks came into the desert, many centuries ago, to find a more direct way of communicating with God. And in the olden days, the monks found it. Because here in the desert there is not the distraction of the towns and the cities. Here, one can concentrate. But things are changing. Today, we are so busy with tourists all the time that we are losing our sense of the desert. The whole special nature of this area is disappearing. There are too many people here." And he quoted to me the archetypal words of the fourth-century hermit Onuphrios: "He who holds intercourse with his fellow man will never be able to speak with the angels."

Since he has been archbishop, Damianos has had little time for talk with the angels. He travels continuously throughout his bishopric and to Greece, ordering the affairs of his monasteries and maneuvering for independence with the authorities. He was especially upset about the four-lane highway that the Israeli administration began building from the eastern Sinai coast up to Santa Katerina. This would have made what was once a tough two-day jeep ride through deep ravines into a two-hour jaunt for anything on four wheels. And like the personnel of the Israel Society for the Protection of Nature Field Station nearby, he was deeply concerned lest the influx of tourists attracted by the easy access completely ruin the area.

The gravel bed for that road is still there, a cruel scar slashing through the dramatic scenery. It has not been asphalted—Israel signed peace with Egypt before that stage of construction—but the monks still fear that the Egyptians might complete the road, particularly if President Sadat fulfills his promise to the world to build a joint mosque-synagogue-church on top of Mount Sinai. This proposal has incensed the monks, not the least because of the publicity and tourism that it would attract. But most galling of all to them is the fact that they were not consulted on the idea. While the Israelis at least informed and usually consulted them on developments in the area, this time the monks find they have been ignored altogether. The Sadat proposal is thus a possibly devastating blow to their authority in the area.

Their ire is all the more understandable considering their sense of historical perspective. The monastery has been there for thirteen hundred years, long before the present nation-states of Egypt and Israel. Its generations of monks have outlived empires and conquerors, and today's monks have every reason to believe that their successors will outlive whatever regimes may take authority over the area in the next thirteen hundred years. In the year 3300, they reason, Santa Katerina Monastery will still be flourishing, whereas the nation-states of today may have disappeared within who knows what new configuration. Where the Beduin consider themselves outside the Mideast conflict, the monks of Santa Katerina consider themselves above it, part of a tradition that has outlived any who dared challenge its authority.

One must hope that Sadat will not put his plan into effect, though he is a man who has proven to what extent he can keep his word. For Mount Sinai is a truly holy place only to the Christians. Both the Moslems and the Jews see it as a place where holy things have occurred, but no more. The Beduin of the area venerate the tombs of their sheikhs and holy men far more than Mount Sinai, while the Jews regard Sinai more as a place through which they have passed than a place to be revered in itself. Physically, moreover, such a project as that envisioned by Sadat would be extremely difficult to carry out. There is no room for such a structure on the peak of Mount Sinai itself; it could conceivably be built on the broad expanse in the center of the mountain known as Farsh Eliahu, but if so it would irrevocably ruin the serenity and magic of that very special mountain. Not only Archbishop Damianos, but many others who know, love, and venerate Mount Sinai, trust that this one time, President Sadat will not keep his word but will prefer instead the special holiness of the place that stems from its very isolation.

Though Sadat's plans for Mount Sinai may be doubtful, his plans for the rest of the Sinai resound with the same determination that led him into the peacemaking process. He is intent on what he calls Egypt's "third revolution." The first revolution, he says, was the coup d'état by which Gamal Abdul Nasser overthrew the Egyptian monarchy in 1952. The second, what Sadat calls "the corrective revolution," was the power struggle in which he established his claim to Egypt's leadership after Nasser's death. Now, he says, the time has come for the "green revolution," in which he intends to tackle head-on Egypt's population and agricultural problems. The peace agreement with Israel has brought about a radical change in Egypt's attitude to the Sinai. Where before it was a buffer zone between the two countries, Egypt now sees it as an area of new possibilities in agriculture and development.

Ninety-six percent of Egypt's population lives on four percent of its land—in the long narrow strip of the Nile Valley, which has been called the "heart line of Egypt." On either side of the valley is desert. Though desert agriculture schemes have been introduced over the last decade, the land regained for food production has been offset by land lost in other areas to desert encroachment and by bad irrigation practices in the Nile Delta, which have waterlogged the soil and led to a rapid increase in salinization. Egypt's cities are choking with people as peasant farmers abandon their meager holdings along the Nile to search out a better living in construction or industry. Over half of Egypt's imports are now basic foods. Heavy taxes on agricultural profits have combined with government subsidies of basic foods in the urban centers to increase the migration into the towns. Thus, one of Sadat's top priorities is population dispersal and the agricultural revolution that would make this possible.

The return of the Sinai to Egypt, together with the network of agricultural settlements set up since 1967 by Israel—in particular along the Mediterranean coast—provide Sadat with an excellent opportunity to set the green revolution in motion. Egyptian planners are already working on a tunnel beneath the Suez Canal to bring water, fuel, electricity, and communications from the heartland of Egypt into the Sinai Peninsula. Some planners talk of a series of towns and villages throughout the Sinai, though this seems an unlikely prospect for the near future. It is clearly in Egypt's interest to take over and expand the farms to be abandoned by the Israeli settlers, but widening this network to the interior of the Sinai would be prohibitively expensive. The Nile is indeed a plenteous water supply, but it would make more sense both economically and technologically to divert its waters to the desert lands near to it rather than overland and under the canal into the Sinai interior.

Israeli scientists and planners, excited by Sadat's announcement of his third revolution, have envisioned a new era of joint Egyptian-Israeli projects in desert agriculture, with the two countries pooling ideas and resources on water use and management, on antidesertification methods, on nonconventional energy sources, and on the development of new specifically desert food and industrial crops, such as the jojoba oil bean. But for the meantime, it seems that Egypt will prefer to go it alone and that any exchange of ideas and information will take place at a quieter and more discreet level than some Israeli planners excitedly dream of. As the Egyptian officer in the United Nations buffer zone said, the foundations of peace have been established, but it will take time until peace in all its aspects of coexistence and cooperation will come into being.

Though the green revolution may be a long and slow one, the face of the Sinai in peacetime will eventually be very different from its wartime appearance. The grace of those years between planning and execution may enable the Egyptians to develop the Sinai wisely and respectfully, with methods adapted to the desert itself.

The Negev, however, has received no such time grace. Within a few years, it is destined to disappear forever under the bulldozer and the tank. For the sad fact remains that although Israel is now at peace with Egypt, it remains on a war footing with the rest of the Arab world—a hostile front headed by Syria, Libya, Iraq, Saudi Arabia, Iran, Jordan, and the Palestine Liberation Organization, and backed by the rest of the Arab world. Israel's army must train and the Negev desert is now the only area large enough to accommodate it.

Israel's armed forces grew more than fourfold between 1967 and 1979, and most of this increase was absorbed in the Sinai.

By 1982, this army will have to withdraw to the Negev. In addition to three major military airfields, to be dismantled in the Sinai and rebuilt in the Negev, the Israel Defense Forces will have to move some seventy-five thousand tons of equipment and almost four thousand vehicles out of the Sinai and into the Negev. Seventy-nine military camps and military installations, including two major early-warning stations, will be dismantled. Fifty new military camps will be set up in the Negev, which is just over one-quarter the size of the Sinai; hundreds of miles of new roads, water pipes, and high-tension cables will be built and installed, and some ninety million cubic meters of earth will be moved.

The Israeli army's increase in size has been more than matched by the increasing sophistication of its weaponry. The new weapons require far larger spaces than before for training maneuvers, so that vast tracts of the Negev will be closed off as firing and practice ranges. The International Institute of Strategic Studies reckons that Israel has over three thousand tanks and many thousand armored-personnel carriers and long-range howitzers. Training grounds for this arsenal may take up two-thirds of the Negev.

Inevitably, army maneuvers change the desert into the barren desolation of popular imagination. Within months, the natural vegetation and animal and bird life of an army training area is depleted, trampled under tank treads, blown up by howitzers. Ugly scars of jeep and tank tracks slash through the landscape, crisscrossing as time goes on to create a maze of tramped-down desert soil in which no creatures can live. Under such an assault, the fragile desert ecosystem breaks down completely. The living desert becomes a dead one. This is the tragic but necessary fate of much of the Negev in the near future.

The rest of the Negev, meanwhile, is gearing up for an economic boom. The influx of military personnel, some of whom will be posted permanently in the Negev together with their families, will be a rapid and welcome boon to the development towns, especially to Mitzpe Ramon in the central Negev, which will be near a major airfield. The influx of construction workers and technical personnel for the three years that it will take to construct the new infrastructure will boost the economies of the tiny desert townships, and the planned network of new highways and renovated roads will make Israel's once-distant wildernesses accessible to transport and industry. Plans for the industrial development of the Negev are being pushed ahead, with special emphasis on chemical industries, whose pollution can devastate the desert ecosystem as rapidly and efficiently as army maneuvers. The Negev's future has become a planner's dream—and a conservationist's nightmare. Areas currently protected as nature reserves will be drastically reduced in size. Many conservationists fear that by the year 2000, the reserves will be only small islands to remind people of what this desert once was, pockets of live desert in the midst of a military-industrial complex.

Peace, not war, may finally lead to the Negev's being conquered. Its rich spaces will be circumscribed. Where then, will we find this desert's vistas of time and space, the grandeur of color and form, the stillness of rock and the sudden movement of wildlife, the silence of the midday heat and the howl of the wind at sunset as it curls into the mountains and gullies? Where will we escape the sound of trucks laboring uphill, the booms of artillery practice on the plains, the litter and garbage dumps of civilization, the ravages of industrial pollution?

In Israel, we have made peace with Egypt. Yet, in the way of all countries, developed and developing, it seems that we too will not make peace with the land. I welcome peace with Egypt and rejoice in it, as do all who prefer words to blood, the handshake to the bayonet thrust. Yet each one of us in Israel carries within us the special, personal price of peace. For me, that price is the Negev.

I mourn the death of a desert.

Selected Bibliography

Camus, Albert. *The Myth of Sisyphus*. New York: Vintage, 1955.

Doughty, C. M. *Travels in Arabia Deserta*. London: Jonathan Cape, 1928.

Evenari, Michael; Shanan, Leslie; and Tadmor, Naphtali. *The Negev: Challenge of a Desert*. Cambridge: Harvard University Press, 1971.

Glueck, Nelson. *Deities and Dolphins*. New York: Farrar, Straus and Giroux, 1971.

Herbert, Frank. *Dune*. New York: Ace, 1965.

Jarvis, Major C. S. *Three Deserts*. London: J. Murray, 1936.

——*Desert and Delta*. London: J. Murray, 1938.

Kazantzakis, Nikos. *Journeyings*. New York: Little Brown, 1975.

Lawrence, T. E. *The Seven Pillars of Wisdom*. London: Jonathan Cape, 1935.

Leopold, Aldo. *A Sand County Almanac*. New York: Ballantine, 1970.

McPhee, John. *Encounters with the Archdruid*. New York: Farrar, Straus and Giroux, 1971.

Meshel, Zeev. *Southern Sinai*. Tel Aviv: Kibbutz HaMeuhad, 1976.

Moorhouse, Geoffrey. *The Fearful Void*. London: Hodder and Stoughton, 1975.

Palmer, E. H. *The Desert of the Exodus*. New York: Harper, 1872.

Schumacher, E. F. *Small Is Beautiful*. New York: Harper & Row, 1973.

van der Post, Laurens. *A Far-Off Place*. New York: Harvest/HBJ, 1978.

Waddell, Helen. *The Desert Fathers*. London: Fontana, 1936.

Woolley, Sir Charles Leonard; and Lawrence, T. E. *The Wilderness of Zin*. London: Jonathan Cape, 1936.

Free

MP 6K